"The challenge to business in the coming decade
will be to operate in a world where
trends of the past
no longer predict the future."
—Jay W. Forrester, MIT

New Traditions in Business

SPIRIT and LEADERSHIP in the 21st CENTURY

New Traditions in Business

SPIRIT and LEADERSHIP in the 21st CENTURY

Authors

Willis Harman, Ph.D.

Michael L. Ray, Ph.D.

Herman B. Maynard, Jr.

Jim Channon

William C. Miller

Peter M. Senge, Ph.D.

Terry Mollner, Ed.D.

Robert H. Rosen, Ph.D

Juanita Brown

Cynthia F. Barnum

David R. Gaster

Charles F. Kiefer

Carol Sanford

John W. Thompson, Ph.D.

Ken Blanchard, Ph.D.

Editor: John R. Renesch

STERLING
& STONE,
INC.
New Leaders Press

San Francisco, CA

New Traditions in Business:
Spirit and Leadership in the 21st Century
John Renesch, Editor

For further information, address the publisher:
New Leaders Press, an affiliate of Sterling & Stone, Inc.,
1000 Chestnut Street, Suite 14C, San Francisco, CA 94109.

ISBN: 0-9630390-0-8

Library of Congress Catalog Card Number: 91-753C7

Printed in the United States of America
9   8   7   6   5   4   3   2   1

Dedication

*This book is dedicated
to the men and women in the business community
who possess a vision for a better world
and the courage to evoke positive change—
helping to establish new traditions
that enable businesses to thrive
while being responsible to and
for the whole of humanity.*

Table of Contents

Part II

Acknowledgments

David Garfinkel served as project manager for this book, coordinating contributions from each author and generally supporting them in completing manuscripts on time. David is president of San Francisco-based GW Systems and has added some of his own personal reflections to the end of these acknowledgments. Pat Barrentine, a key member of *The New Leaders* newsletter team, has also been a valuable member of the team in addition to referring the publisher to her daughter, Marcia Barrentine, who produced the cover.

A special acknowledgment goes to Jim Channon, one of our coauthors who also offered some key design concepts for the book's cover. Jim produced the magical photograph used on the cover. Paul Clemens, and his team at Blue Dolphin Press, Inc., provided important wisdom as well as production and set-up for galleys.

Much appreciation goes to the authors—the men and women who shared the vision of this work and who joined with us as partners in completing this book. These people are truly visionaries, and we are very proud to have had the privilege of publishing their work.

Those who buy and read this book are playing a key role in the "awakening" of the business community worldwide. Some of you will be leaders, providing inspiration to hundreds of others in a transition to a better way. Some of you will be followers, lending your own unique perspective to the tasks at hand. And some of you will be observers, perhaps even pessimistic bystanders. Each of you will be doing your own part in the unfolding of our collective future.

Thank you all! To those who contributed to the content of this book, those who helped in the publishing of it, and those for whom it was produced. And, finally, thanks to our inspiration—that spirit that is ready to be acknowledged in all of us, whether we are at home or at the office.

It has been a true pleasure,

John R. Renesch, Editor

Additional Thoughts

As project manager for this book, I was privileged to work directly with these authors over the past year and would like to share some personal reflections.

This book contains a valuable collection of wisdom, viewpoints, predictions, and practical ideas, and I truly hope that in enjoying and benefiting from these chapters that you, the reader, will always keep in mind that each of these was written by a person, a human being.

I know in my own life it becomes far too easy to pigeonhole names, affiliations, and categories of authors and put on the back burner the importance of the individuality of the special human being from whose fingers or throat these words came.

I write these words for a very deliberate reason. In my work with writers over the years, I have known a fine cross section of personalities and intellects in business, technology, general-interest journalism, and fiction. The popular stereotypes of writers are somewhat overblown. Still, few I have worked with have ever come close to fitting the characterization "larger than life" for me.

Until now, that is. The people whose words grace the pages of this book not only teach and preach a visionary way of doing business, but, in my experience, they *live* it. For example, Jim Channon was not only a delight to work with but, in my conversations with him, I learned things of such value about consciousness and its revered role in the lives of some of the heads of the world's largest business organizations—to whom he consults—that I literally sleep better nights. (I hope you will gain inner peace from the thoughts of some of the authors as well.)

There was a gentleness in the confidence, and a compassion in the authority, of the people I worked with. As Terry Mollner was discussing with me some of his recent travels and his ideas for his chapter, I found myself in the midst of a conversation I'd been longing to have for years. Here was a person who commanded the context and had the knowledge to speak easily and articulately about things I had felt for a long time were happening in the world and had gone unreported in the media and most business organizations. And yet, he was as down-to-earth as a college buddy, a next-door neighbor, or a long-lost friend.

Dear reader, if I sound a tad sentimental, I am. Many of us who have high hopes for business truly deserve this book. May it serve you well.

David Garfinkel, Project Manager

Introduction

Fifteen of the foremost visionaries who are currently addressing the emerging, revised role for the business community have come together in this anthology to offer their various viewpoints. Each one of these distinguished authors presents his or her own unique perspective while focusing on a particular element of the transition that is currently under way, challenging business leaders around the globe.

These ideas are not reserved for the multinational organization—they are not the exclusive domain of the global corporation. The issues addressed in these pages are of equal value to the small regional enterprise and its community of stakeholders (employees, owners, customers, vendors, and local citizenry). The recognition that our society has become extremely complex and that everything is somehow connected to everything else can be a valuable realization for everyone in business, whether they or their company are engaged in international trade or offering products to a small community.

While each author in this book possesses a unique style of writing, and addresses different issues, two common themes run through this collection of works. The first is the connection that all human beings have with one another, recognizing that each of us is engaged in many social systems as well as the "system of systems." Nothing happens that doesn't affect us to some degree, and everything we do (or don't do) affects everything else. We are not always able to choose the systems in which we participate—the situations are mostly evolutionary. Each of us is part of a relationship system (romantic, friends, family), a generational system, a profession or trade system, a national culture, a religious or spiritual system, an ethnic tradition, and many more, including being a part of humanity— a very large system indeed!

The second thread of commonality that runs through these chapters is that each of us is responsible for our own actions and the effect we have on the whole. This responsibility might be obvious for those who accept interconnectedness—after all, it seems like a natural progression. If everything we do affects the whole, then we can recognize our responsibility *to* the whole. We may not want to—we may not like this conclusion, but the responsibility is there whether we like it or not.

The primary objective of this book is to support the awakening process in the world of business—the "call for action" by responsible individuals in the professional and executive ranks. More and more people are beginning to recognize that long-held beliefs about how business is supposed to be do not need to go unchallenged. Growing incongruence between personal ideals and values and the traditional exploitation process to which one is subjected in the business world is causing greater numbers of awakening souls to question old behaviors, challenge old assumptions, and take a stand for their own self-respect—their own integrity.

It seems as if the human spirit is defending itself against the tyranny of past attitudes such as, "Anything is okay so long as profits go up." Using short-term economic measures as the standard for policies in how businesses treat their employees, their customers, and the environment is rapidly becoming outmoded.

Each of the following chapters can be read as if it were a short book in itself. Much of what each author could express in his or her own book is contained in his or her individual chapter.

The first part of the book deals largely with context. Willis Harman provides us with a historic overview bringing us to this modern milestone in the evolution of our species. Michael Ray focuses on what is meant by this "new paradigm business," sharing much of what he has learned since launching the first course of its type in a major business school (Stanford University has been offering Dr. Ray's course, New Paradigm Business, since January 1990).

Du Pont executive Herman Maynard shares his research into human consciousness and its current transition during this historic time. Jim Channon and William Miller both address the issue of spirituality and its role in the workplace of the future. Spirit could be described as the context of all contexts.

In the second part of this anthology, the structure and content of the new organization is addressed first by Peter Senge, with his "learning organization." Terry Mollner looks at the new corporation from the perspective of "community"—similar to native tribal cultures. Robert Rosen examines the structure of a "healthy" company—expanding the definition of a word we might normally associate with medical well-being or profitability of the enterprise.

Juanita Brown makes her own comparisons between traditional corporate life and developing a sense of community in the workplace, and Cynthia Barnum shares her international background in offering three steps for "going global." British author David Gaster addresses the need for new leadership from today's business visionaries, and Charles Kiefer examines the requirements for leaders to bring about organizations that empower people to the fullest.

Taking a leadership perspective of changing paradigms, Carol Sanford examines structural thinking, and John Thompson looks ahead to corporate leadership in the next century. Finally, Ken Blanchard offers his views of ethics in the current American workplace and his five principles for ethical power.

Some of these chapters will require significant focus and attention—some make for easier reading. However, they all offer valuable points of view and "leading edge" wisdom for the forward-thinking business executive—whether you be an entrepreneur, product manager, vice president, or chairman of the board.

It has been a privilege to work with these authors and to be part of an enterprise that brings so much talent together. I trust it will serve you well.

Respectfully,

John R. Renesch, Editor

Part I

These early chapters provide an overview of mankind's evolution to date, which provides a context in which we may be able to appreciate the absolutely historic opportunities that are presenting themselves to the business community.

WILLIS HARMAN, Ph.D., is one of the leading futurists of our time. He is president of the Institute of Noetic Sciences, which he joined in 1977 at the invitation of its founder, astronaut Edgar Mitchell. He has served as a regent of the University of California, is emeritus professor of Engineering-Economic Systems at Stanford University, and for sixteen years was senior social scientist at SRI International. He wrote *Global Mind Change, the Promise of the Last Years of the Twentieth Century* (1988) and coauthored *Creative Work* (1990) with IBM executive John Hormann. Dr. Harman is a founding trustee of the World Business Academy and serves on its Board of Governors.

John Renesch, publisher of *The New Leaders* newsletter and editor of this book, assisted in the writing of this chapter. Renesch is also managing director of the World Business Academy.

1

21st-Century Business: A Background for Dialogue

Willis Harman

Few would doubt that the modern world—and business in particular—is passing through some fairly major transition, perhaps even a fundamental transformation. What is the nature of this transition, and what does it imply for business leadership?

Of all of our society's institutions, business seems to be the best prepared to respond to the many changes we are facing. The modern business organization, developed to respond promptly to changing market forces, is today's most adaptive institution. Institutions that have historically served as society's leaders—the churches, governments, and our learning institutions—have become too cumbersome for today's modern pace, where constant change is the norm. Does business then have an obligation to take a leadership role since it is the most capable of our present-day institutions to deal with changes, transitions, even transformation in our modern world?

Before we start to address that question, let us examine the nature of this transition we are experiencing. Those who perceive modern society to be passing through a fundamental transformation tend to emphasize three bits of evidence. One is the global dilemmas that are not resolvable through the usual approaches—technological "fixes," new management practices, and legislative programs—that are "pushing" the system toward needed fundamental change. The second bit of evidence is the shifting value emphases that are "pulling" us toward an uncertain future. The third clue lies in the various manifestations of a fundamental shift in the worldview underlying the whole structure of modern society. We will explore each of these three briefly.

The Global Dilemmas

The Bruntland Commission Report, *Our Common Future* (1987), and the U.S. Government's *Global 2000* (1980) essentially contain the same message. The world is beset with a complex of global problems including environmental degradation, resource depletion, toxic chemical concentrations, man-made climate change, chronic hunger and poverty, species extinction, and the threat of modern military powers to obliterate whole populations in the name of "national security." Most of these problems are becoming progressively more severe; they are highly interconnected with one another, with industrialization and with population concentration; without major changes in the present trends, these problems will become intolerably grievous by early in the next century, just a few years from now! These problems are probably no longer solvable within the framework of the established, traditional, and industrial order. Therein lies the dilemma. The price of bringing about the necessary system change to resolve these problems and support "sustainable development" seems too high. But, the price may be even higher if the change does not take place. Hence, a dilemma exists.

Changing Values

There is a "change of mind" taking place in the modern world that is reflected in demographic survey data, in the new values emphasis of the women's movement, in the ecological, peace, and alternative lifestyles movements, in the Green political movements in various countries, and in the suddenly rising interest in various "12 step" programs for dealing with addictions and co-dependency. This change of mind is characterized by a repudiation of the competitive, exploitive materialism and consumerism of modern society, with an increased emphasis on alternative values. These values include improved quality of relationships, cooperation, caring and nurturing, oneness of humanity, social justice, humane, ecological and spiritual values, as well as respect and caring for the other creatures on the planet.

One of the most interesting of current social phenomena is the rapid spreading of the group-help approach to problems of addiction, which has expanded from being the most effective way to deal with alcoholism (Alcoholics Anonymous) to being a broad social movement in its own right.

A key component of the AA approach to supporting the recovering alcoholic is the "12 step" program. In brief, the 12 steps include admitting powerlessness over alcohol (or whatever the addiction is) and admitting that life as an alcoholic has become unmanageable; recognizing the help possible from "a Power greater than ourselves" to aid in the restoration of sanity; taking one's own "moral inventory"; admitting problems to others; trying to make amends to those persons harmed in the past; seeking contact with God "as we understand Him"; and, finally, carrying the message of spiritual awakening to other alcoholics in a mutual support system.

This approach has proven so successful with the treatment of alcoholism that it has been extended, over the past decade, to other forms of addiction—including all forms of chemical dependency, food abuse, gambling, sexual compulsions, and smoking. In addition, recognition of the mutual interdependence that occurs where a relationship involves addiction has led to the creation of support groups for spouses and children of alcoholics as well as for other forms of co-dependence. The 12-step approach has recently been extended to include our collective "addiction" to consumerism in the Western world. Once people sense the possibility of self-determination and freedom in one area of their lives, they are likely to want to extend it to the rest. Thus, this approach is part of a broad and growing self-liberation movement.

Among the many social phenomena that convey and denote the shifting values emphasis, one particular transition stands out—the women's movement. Beyond being a movement of women, asserting women's rights, it stresses the benefits and importance of a feminine point of view for all humans. All of us possess masculine and feminine characteristics. The feminine focus involves an emphasis on such values as caring, nurturing, cooperating, and creating. It focuses on a perception of relationships rather than things, of wholeness over parts, and the authenticity of inner knowing. It relates to the liberation of the feminine energies in the male as well as the female.

A counterpart liberation movement is taking place within the developing world: the "sleeping giant" is awakening. Those who have accepted the role of privation, inferiority, and servility in the past are less and less willing to do so in the future. In recent years there has been growing insistence on a different international economic order and the exploration of alternative development paths. The various cultures of the indigenous peoples around the world, almost stamped out by colonialism and modernism, are showing a resurgence. There is growing appreciation of an ecologically wholesome relationship to Nature that is embodied in the spiritual traditions of these native peoples.

If these attitudes continue to gain strength, the thrust will not be toward Western industrial monoculture around the globe, but rather toward an ecology of diverse cultures, each with its own interpretation of human development, societal goals, and ultimate meaning. The thrust will be toward a world system that tends to support rather than diminish, bias against, or thwart this diversity.

Worldview

Throughout the industrialized world there are widespread indications of a shift in worldview. In brief, this is characterized by two features. One is an emphasis on interconnectedness and wholeness—a growing awareness that, although we may compete, we are nonetheless each part of a unity, so that no one "wins" unless we all do. The other is a shifting attitude toward our inner, subjective experience—affirming inner wisdom, authority, and resources—challenging the scientific materialism that was so dominant in the earlier part of the century.

Discerning persons have long been aware that there has been something wrong with the scientific picture of reality. Almost by definition it fails to include human intention, conscious awareness, and that broad spectrum of "exceptional abilities" that appear to be scattered throughout the population.

For a long time Western culture has been trying to manage a society based on two incompatible pictures of reality—one "scientific" and the other in some sense "spiritual." The former tended to deny the spiritual, and the latter found science irrelevant to the important questions of life. This contradictory dynamic should have suggested to us that something was wrong somewhere.

The Danish philosopher Sören Kierkegaard opined that there are two ways of being fooled—to believe something that *isn't* so, and to refuse to believe something that *is* so. One of the things we have been most reluctant to believe is that we are all hypnotized by our culture so that we experience reality in the "culturally approved" way. This is true for us in the modern world just as much as it is true for those cultures that we term primitive or pre-scientific. This is a humbling observation, but essential to the understanding of the present social change forces—that our modern, scientific concept of reality is in some sense arbitrary and parochial.

The practical importance of this shift in basic premises may not be immediately apparent. Modern industrial society, like every other society in history, rests on a set of largely tacit, basic assumptions about who we are, what kind of a universe we are in, and what is ultimately important to us. The scientific materialism that so confidently held forth its answers to these questions a couple of generations ago is now a dying orthodoxy. Its basic positivistic and reductionistic premises are being replaced by a new set of beliefs that include increased faith in reason guided by deep intuition. In other words, a "respiritualization" of society is taking place that is more experiential and less fundamentalist than most of the historically familiar forms of structured religion. Such a change in basic assumptions must inevitably be accompanied by a long-term shift in value emphases and priorities. With these changes in our basic premises, all of our society's institutions can be expected to go through major changes, including the industrial, economic, and financial institutions in particular.

Nature of the Transformation

In using the term "transformation" to describe this transition period, we do not mean simply *change*. We do not mean *big change* or even rather *radical change*. People living today have all experienced rapid, life-transforming technological change throughout their lives. We are not referring to more change of a familiar sort, but to trend-breaking change of a kind that is unknown in our life experience—a shift of an entire society's mind-set.

Perhaps the closest comparison we can make is with the change that took place in Western Europe in the 17th century. This period was essentially the transition from medieval to modern times. It amounted to a shift in the basic perception of reality. The world perceived by a person living in Western Europe in the year 1600 was still the world of the Middle Ages. By 1700, the educated person would perceive—literally—a different reality, one with faith in human progress and values not too different from those characterizing our current modern society. This rapid and fundamental shift in the perception of reality eventually transformed every institution and way of life throughout most of the world.

The defining characteristics of modern society—centrality of the economic and technology-centered institutions, steadily rising demand for democracy and equity, unbridled national sovereignty, and the supremacy of the scientific definition of "reality"—were more or less set in place by the end of the 17th century. By now these characteristics have influenced practically all other societies around the globe. They account for the present dominance of Western culture. They are also the source of the global dilemmas we now face.

Confidence and reliance upon the "reality" of empirical science has grown steadily since then. Science has been astoundingly successful at providing the power to "predict and control" in the physical world, as modern technological prowess attests. Yet, by the latter part of the 20th century there have been unmistakable signs that, however useful science might be for some purposes, its growth has had a serious negative effect on our understanding of values. This effect has undermined the common religious base of values and replaced it with a kind of moral relativism. A kind of pseudo-values, economic and technical values, material progress, efficiency, and productivity filled the vacuum. Decisions that would affect the lives of people around the globe, and generations to come, were decided on the basis of short-term economic considerations. The "technological imperative" to develop and apply any technology that could turn a profit or destroy an enemy endangered both the life-support systems of the planet and human civilization.

Thus the "new heresy" came to be the spreading belief that reality is not found in the reductionistic scientific worldview any more than it was found in dogmatic theology. As the modern perception of reality differed from the medieval, so a growing band of individuals today are betting their lives on a different picture of reality than that of conventional science. It is not just that some "New Age" values are loose in the land; rather, a competing picture of reality infuses holistic health care approaches, new concepts of business management, and people seeking to replace the lost meaning in their lives. As the "scientific heresy" affected every institution in 18th-century society, so the "new heresy" will do the same into the 21st century, but far more rapidly.

25

We shall take two examples of the consequences of this shift: (a) the emerging system form, a "third way" that is "beyond capitalism and socialism," and (b) the meaning of intuition and the potentialities it suggests, which are far different in the emerging paradigm than in the scientific paradigm that still reigns supreme.

The Emerging "Third Way"

Terry Mollner suggests that emerging out of the new picture of reality is a new system form, "beyond capitalism and socialism." In fact, he claims that the chief reason Japan has been doing so well in the world market is precisely because it has gone farther in the direction of this new form than either the United States or the socialist countries.

Basic to this "third way" is a shift from a Material Age worldview to a Relationship Age worldview. The former assumes that the universe is a collection of *separate parts*, each of which *competes* for its own self-interest in relation to all other things. The later assumes that the universe is a vast number of *connected parts*, each of which *cooperates* with all other parts in the interest of the whole. Only secondarily does it cooperate or compete in the interest of itself or any subgroup of parts. The system based on Relationship Age worldview—the "next phase of social evolution"—is a society where people *freely* choose to give priority to the interests of the society as a whole and act upon those priorities through a process of cooperation rather than competition. The most mature examples of this new system form are the worker-owned cooperatives of the Mondragon community in Spain and the Central Union in Poland. These are basically familial organizations. People choose to produce high-quality products and services because they enjoy doing so in a familial grouping and because they see it as a service to humanity rather than primarily for personal profit. Management is hierarchical for efficiency, but with a moral consensus.

The "third way" is not simply a device that can be transported and operated anywhere. It is based on a different picture of reality from the reductionistic, competitive picture of the West and only functions well within that new context.

Intuitive Leadership and Sound Business

Intuitive leadership is a term that has come into vogue only recently. In fact, it is only in the last decade or so that tough-minded male executives have confessed to using intuition in their decision making. What is meant by "intuitive leadership"? Why are we suddenly talking about it? Is this another fad like T-groups, MBO, or Quality Circles?

Intuitive leadership is more than simply old-style leadership with some intuition added in to guide the corporate decision. It is leadership that takes into account both (a) the executives' appreciation of the inner resources that are available but often not used and (b) the changes in institutions and society that are accompanying the "awakening" of employees and the public at large. The term "awakening" is used to describe the general phenomenon whereby people are becoming aware that they no longer have to accept their adopted beliefs, beliefs that they developed or accepted throughout most of their lives. These beliefs can include belief in the inferiority of certain ethnic or gender groups, belief in the sacrosanctity of economic customs and business practices (even if they are demonstrably not good for people or the planet), belief in powerlessness before the "big system," or belief in the limited extent of one's own ability to create what one wants.

In view of these changes, what is sound business for the future? What do these changes mean to business people? Of one thing we can be sure: business life will be replete with challenges. Some of these challenges will stem from the global dilemmas mentioned earlier, with growing recognition of the role business has unwittingly played in accelerating modern society's race toward self-destruction. Some of these challenges will stem from the changing attitudes of employees and the general public—the customers. The new environment for business will emphasize innovation and will be highly competitive. To prosper in such an environment, a business firm will need to attract and hold its most creative people. To do that, businesses will have to provide a work environment that fosters creativity development.

Developing intuitive leadership in the future will not be a luxury or a passing fad; it will be the heart of business. The challenges will be great. It will be necessary to deal effectively with the increasing complexity, interconnectedness, and systemic nature of the economic system. There is both good news and bad news. The bad news is that there will be persistent problems of mediocrity, debt, trade balance, global dilemmas, and worker morale. The good news is that we have inner resources we haven't been using—untapped resources that are quite capable of dealing with these problems.

Thus "intuition" is not just a new gimmick in management decision making. Intuition is a code word for a necessary transformation of business—indeed, of global society.

New Concepts of Management

Corporations and other organizations are increasingly viewed, not as hierarchical structures fitting a traditional organization chart, but as adaptable organisms, made up of more or less autonomous smaller organisms and existing in and interacting with a larger whole. In this organic-system view, organizational purpose is not chosen arbitrarily by select members of the organization but is in large part "given" by the larger system. When the organization plays its part, it receives support and nurturing from the greater whole, similar to the way an organ in a healthy body receives the nourishment it needs without having to work especially hard to survive. The critical strategic question is not how to gain advantage but how to discern purpose and meaning.

Management was once defined as the direction of resources (including human) to accomplish a predetermined task; it is now having more to do with empowering individuals to respond creatively to a changing situation. Management was the wielding of power; now, it is about empowering. As stated above, intuition is becoming increasingly honored in manage-

28

ment; alignment around a shared vision and purpose is a recognized characteristic of the creative organization. Many management training seminars these days are teaching the power of holding a vivid inner image of a goal to bring about a desired result. Participants are cautioned not to believe in any limits to the power of mind to accomplish this—since any limits we believe in will surely be there.

In other leadership development workshops, executives learn that all individuals can discover in themselves a deep sense of purpose. The new concept of management involves honoring that purpose, allowing it full play in the organization, and relying on the motivation associated with it. An emerging form of leadership is replacing traditional management practices. Leading by inspiring, supporting, and the employment of other so-called feminine qualities will be the new style of managing.

A leading executive development seminar teaches that we are not separate individuals as we may have assumed. At some deeper level our minds interconnect, and that is why no one of us can really win unless we all do. Executives are taught in such seminars that the inhibiting effect of fear (of ridicule, of criticism, of failure, of success) can be overcome. One can learn to trust the total environment in such a way that all experience is accepted as valuable feedback, and there is nothing to fear. "Contextual management" will replace fear-oriented methods of getting results.

Implications for Business

And so we circle back to the question with which we started. Are the present changes in business and organizations a fad or a passing trend that may last a while and then be replaced by another new idea? Or are these changes part of a much broader pattern representing a fundamental shift in which the value priorities of the entire society are going through reassessment (as is the underlying image of reality) and even the purpose of the corporation is being redefined? There is much contemporary evidence to support the latter view.

Because of the fundamental nature of the transformation, the task of anticipating the shape of business in the 21st century is analogous to trying to forecast the shape of the modern business organization from the mid-17th century. Yet, we can be aware of the transition in a way that our 17th-century European counterparts could not. We can observe the forerunner changes taking place and can imagine what the business organization would be like if those kinds of values and outlooks came to prevail.

If intuitive leadership is what is required on the planet, and if business (with its increasing level of democratic participation and shared vision) is the most suitable instrument for creating a positive future, then business will be playing a different role—and that role will be "good business." After all, you can't do good business in a society that is headed toward self-destruction.

If we accept that intuitive leadership is an important key to creating and manifesting a new vision for the '90s, the first (and for some the hardest) thing to recognize is that we don't sit down and figure out what the "new vision" is to be. If there is anything at all to the concept of intuitive leadership, we listen to hear and we *watch* the inner images to see what the new pattern is to be.

The other thing to learn is that manifesting is not the sort of frenetic activity we so often associate with building a business or creating a product. The nature of the universe appears to be such that if we are very clear about the present state (and hence the tension between the two), this very envisioning invites the universe to conspire to manifest the vision.

MICHAEL L. RAY, Ph.D., is the John G. McCoy-Banc One Corporation professor of creativity and innovation and of marketing
at Stanford University's Graduate School of Business. He is a
specialist in creativity, innovation, marketing communication,
advertising, and the behavioral science approach to marketing
problems. He is a social psychologist with extensive experience
in advertising and marketing management and a fellow of the
World Business Academy.

He is author of *Advertising and Communication Management*
(Prentice-Hall, 1982) and editor of *Measurement Readings for
Marketing Research* (American Marketing Association, 1984).
His book (coauthored with Rochelle Myers), *Creativity in Busi-
ness* (Doubleday, 1986, 1989), is based on his Stanford course of
the same name, which has received attention in the *New York
Times*, *Management Review* and *Fortune* and on such televisions
programs as "Donahue," "20/20," and the 1991 PBS series "The
Creative Spirit."

2

The Emerging New Paradigm in Business

Michael L. Ray

Virtually everyone has a working knowledge of the changes occurring in society and in world business. But everyone has somewhat different experiences with these changes. This chapter attempts to establish a common ground. It states the nature of the new paradigm and the shifts it is causing in business.

The Roots of the Present Change

Paradigm (pair-eh-dime) is not a commonly used word. Dictionary definitions tell us that it signifies a pattern, example, or model. But in science the word took on extra significance with the publication of Thomas Kuhn's *The Structure of Scientific Revolutions* in the early 1960s. That significance has now spread to all of society in general and to business in particular.

Kuhn made the point that a field wasn't even a science if it didn't have a paradigm, a set of fundamental assumptions about the nature of the world that were shared by everybody practicing the discipline. That is, everybody practicing physics, chemistry, or biology makes certain assumptions about their world that are so unquestioned, accepted, and ingrained that they are as unnoticed as the air they breathe or the very process of breathing itself. A scientific revolution occurs, says Kuhn, when these fundamental assumptions are questioned and changed—when there is a paradigm shift, when a new paradigm is accepted.

Kuhn and other historians offer the Copernican Revolution of over four hundred years ago as the strongest example of a paradigm shift. In it Copernicus proposed, in opposition to the prevailing Ptolemaic theory that claimed the earth as the center of the universe with the heavens revolving around it, a heliocentric theory in which the earth revolved on its axis and traveled around the sun with other heavenly bodies.

You can imagine how such a paradigm shift would have affected not only science but every part of society and every individual in it. People eventually had to accept that the very ground on which they stood was something that not only was spinning on its axis but was traveling through the heavens with other similar planets around the sun.

Until now that was the greatest paradigm shift in history. But we're told that there is one going on now, and it is even greater and will be more profound in its effects than the Copernican one. As author Huston Smith says:

> *Quietly, irrevocably, something enormous has happened to Western man. His outlook on life and the world has changed so radically that in the perspective of history the twentieth century is likely to rank—with the fourth century, which witnessed the triumph of Christianity, and the seventeenth, which signalled the dawn of modern science—as one of the very few that have instigated genuinely new epochs in human thought. In this change, which is still in process, we of the current generation are playing a crucial but as yet not widely recognized part.*

Of course it took well over a century for Copernicus's ideas to have an effect, even in science. Copernicus probably formulated his ideas in 1530, and they weren't published until 1543 when he was on his deathbed. Eventually they led to Kepler's laws (the first two were published in 1609), Galileo's ideas about the solar system that led to his trial for heresy in 1633, Newton's laws, including the discovery of gravitation (1664-66), and the scientific revolution that is the dominant paradigm of today not only in science but also in every aspect of our culture and everyday life.

The New Paradigm

Around the turn of the present century, however, the materialistic and analytical assumptions of the scientific revolution began to crumble in the face of new theories and findings within science itself. Throughout this century, physicists have had to cope with the ideas of quantum mechanics, chemists with the existence of polymers, biologists with hybrids, ecologists with whole systems, and psychologists with the unconscious. One observer points out that proponents of the old paradigm, as well as people who wouldn't even know what a paradigm was, swept so much under the carpet that they couldn't stand anymore.

The new paradigm that is replacing the old scientific one has many aspects, but its foundation is the notion that consciousness is causal, that the world is as we see it and that the power of the individual psyche is far more vast than we could have previously imagined. To put it into everyday terms, we'll see it when we believe it, or it doesn't exist until we believe it.

The new paradigm realizes that the solidity and stability of the world as represented by Newton's laws have been replaced by quantum theories and findings of a world of infinitesimal particles moving at speeds faster than light in energy fields composed almost totally of empty space. As futurist and economist George Gilder puts it in his book *Microcosm: The Quantum Revolution in Economics and Technology:*

> *The central event of the 20th century is the overthrow of matter. In technology, economics, and the politics of na-*

tions, wealth in the form of physical resources is steadily declining in value and significance. The powers of mind are everywhere ascendant over the brute force of things.

Gilder points out that the scientific shift from matter to energy and thus to mind has already been represented in technology. It is progressing to the point that in the not too distant future it will be possible to put the equivalent of a number of Cray supercomputers on a single chip. And materials represent only 2 percent of the cost of a computer chip.

In telecommunications a few pounds of optical glass fiber carry as much information as a ton of copper did in the past. In fact satellites displace many tons of copper in carrying information.

Intelligence is becoming distributed in society with profound implications for the organization and impact of business. Whereas in the past in consumer electronics people had to depend on large networks for information, it is moving to the point where each household will be able to have its own broadcasting station.

In 1977 virtually all computers were in the form of big mainframes with dumb terminals connected to them. By 1987 only 1 percent of computers were like that; the rest were personal computers and workstations.

In the early days of telecommunications, a whole region would be served by one switching station. In the not too distant future it should be possible to have one in every building.

What all this means is that the power of information has been shifted to the individual. One of the real shocks to those in power in the Soviet Union was that the computer could not be used for centralization. In what many call the age of information, there is substantial evidence that it is becoming the age of individual creativity, because it is in the way the information is used that the power lies. As Gilder puts it:

Sloughing off every layer of macrocosmic apparatus, the computer will ultimately collapse to a pinhead that can respond to the human voice. In this form, human intelligence can be transmitted to any tool or appliance, to any part of our environment. Thus the triumph of the computer does not dehumanize the world; it makes our environment more subject to human will.

The new paradigm is more than just a move to the powers of technology or the individual mind. It is a move to the spirit; to inner qualities such as intuition, will, joy, strength, and compassion.

Spirituality in the new paradigm does not refer to religion but rather to the power of inner wisdom and authority and the connection and wholeness in humanity. In business it is illustrated by the surprising breakthroughs in creativity that occur when people are given responsibility for their actions in new paradigm sorts of organizations. Over and over again, people who never gave any indication of creativity will come through in amazing ways when they are given the opportunity. And in one sense the nature of the new paradigm is simply to give people that opportunity.

The Beginnings of Change in Business

As the dominant paradigm we live with changes from one of scientism to one of honoring the power of consciousness and the human spirit, business has become the main institution of the change. In *Global Mind Change*, futurist Willis Harman puts it this way:

The latter third of this century is a period of fundamental transformation of the modern world, the extent and meaning of which we are only beginning to grasp. . . . The role of business in that transformation is absolutely crucial.

Leaders in business, from very small start-ups to multinational corporations, are recognizing and, more importantly, acting on the shift to the new paradigm. Robert D. Haas, president and CEO of the multinational clothing company Levi Strauss & Company emphasizes the shift from emphasis on matter to emphasis on the human spirit:

The most visible differences between the corporation of the future and its present day counterpart will not be the products they make or the equipment they use—but who will be working, why they will be working, and what work will mean to them.

Perhaps the leading proponent of the new paradigm among large multinational corporations is Jack Welch of General Electric, even though he doesn't use the term. His apparent change in emphasis to his present concern for people and empowerment at GE is almost an icon for the paradigm shift in business. His initial cost cutting and housecleaning earned him the nickname "Neutron Jack," because "GE buildings remained standing but the people disappeared." What he appeared to be doing, however, was moving the giant multinational from a dependence on overly analytic strategy formulation (old paradigm) to a greater concern with opening up people (new paradigm). In a 1989 cover story interview in *Fortune* magazine he said, "The idea of liberation and empowerment for our workforce is not enlightenment—it's a competitive necessity."

That article in *Fortune* highlighted a number of GE product or service lines that were either first or second in domestic or worldwide sales during Welch's tenure there. Later in an interview in *Harvard Business Review*, he once again mirrored the paradigm shift when he commented on the *Fortune* list:

Ten years from now, we want magazines to write about GE as a place where people have the freedom to be creative, a place that brings out the best in everybody—an open, fair place where people have a sense that what they do matters, and where that sense of accomplishment is rewarded in both the pocketbook and the soul.

Management theorist Peter Drucker has seen a great deal of change in business, but he is highlighting what is happening now. He says, "The typical large business 20 years hence will bear little resemblance to the typical manufacturing company, circa 1950, which our textbooks still consider the norm."

As Drucker implies, the old way is just not going to work any more. Polio vaccine discoverer Jonas Salk puts it this way:

"Survival of the world as we know it is not possible. The world will have to be transformed and evolve for continual survival."

Paradigms shift when the old paradigm isn't working anymore. In science, anomalies appear that make it apparent that the old paradigm just is not correct. In business the United States' lack of success in world markets is one bellwether of the need for a new approach. From the 1960s, when such books as Servan-Schrieber's *The American Challenge* trumpeted U.S. dominance, to the 1980s, when such books as Halberstam's *The Reckoning* analyzed its decline, there has been ample evidence that the old paradigm just has not been working in business.

The Nature of the New Paradigm in Business

We are beginning to hear words like vision, alignment, corporate culture, employee ownership, transformation, renewal, stakeholders, and horizontal organization to describe what is happening in business. President Bush talks openly about "that vision thing," and books detailing such concepts as corporate culture and renewal become best sellers. Concern not just with stockholders but with all stakeholders—workers, managers, suppliers, customers, government, community, environment, pressure groups—is adding many concerns beyond simple profit to define the success of the organization.

Although many different observers are talking about the rapid changes in business, they seem to be seeing the same things. For instance, Professor Jerry Wind of the Wharton Business School reported on a consensus among a group of major corporation CEOs as to the characteristics of the organization of the 21st century:

Individual and group empowerment
Learning
Innovative
Flexible
Flatter
Cross functional
Networking between companies
Quality conscious

Customer/market driven
Stakeholders focus (whole set)
Information technology based
Time as a strategic dimension

And Robert Haas of Levi's says his concept of the new business organization, the "corporation without boundaries," would:

Challenge old concepts every day
Treat suppliers and customers as partners
Eliminate the distinction between workers and managers
Redraw the lines between personal and professional concerns
Empower employees so that they can tap fullest potential, take personal responsibility for their contribution, and feel like owners (and will be)
Be technology harnessed, especially information technology
Be global
Compress time as a competitive advantage, be responsive
Have concern for the community
Be non-secretive

In his book *Vanguard Management*, USC's School of Management Professor James O'Toole talks about five principles of excellence that characterize companies practicing vanguard management: stakeholder symmetry, dedication to high purpose, continuous learning, high aim, and moral courage. MIT's Director of Systems Thinking, Peter Senge, outlines the new management style as composed of highly autonomous (and relatively small) business units, few levels of management, profit sharing and employee ownership, and governance structures such as corporate partnerships and internal boards. Others talk about such qualities as attunement, caring, and even love as a characterization of what is happening.

Before discussing some of these individual shifts, it is important to be reminded of the overall paradigm change within which those of us in business are operating. Certain guiding principles from the new paradigm are beginning to govern everything we are doing. The idea that consciousness is not only causal but also infinitely more important than matter is key. People at all levels of business seem to be operating on

40

the basis of three guiding principles: wholeness/interrelationship, inner wisdom, and inner authority.

The overarching purpose of new paradigm business seems to be the enlightenment of all those working within it and the corresponding service to the community surrounding it.

The change is happening on at least the following ten dimensions, and there are many others.

Old Paradigm	New Paradigm
Short-term Goals ———————>	Corporate/Individual Vision
Rigid Culture ———————>	Flexible Culture
Product Orientation —————>	Market Orientation
Internal (to company) Focus —>	External Focus
Regional Emphasis —————>	Global Emphasis
Management Direction ———>	Employee Empowerment
Procedural Bias ——————>	Risk Bias
Analysis Only—————————>	Creativity: Analysis x Intuition
Competition Only —————>	Cooperation, Cocreation, Contribution
Aggressive Values —————>	Harmony, Trust, Honesty, Compassion

Key Issues in Transition

Historically speaking, whenever there is a shift in paradigm, there is chaos. Approaches are tried and abandoned. The shadow side of organizations becomes prominent and then recedes. What are initially thought to be panaceas produce only limited value in the long run. Theory fails in practice. What works in practice for one organization fails for others. The keepers of the old paradigm resist or are unable to cope with the new one. What could be a smooth evolution turns into a seemingly necessary but somewhat dysfunctional revolution.

In the midst of all this there are key issues that must be kept in mind as the transition occurs. The seven that are discussed below come from meetings and retreats of the World Business Academy as well as Stanford's New Paradigm Business course. We have not come to any final conclusions on any of these issues, but they do seem to be pivotal for business in this period of moving toward the new paradigm.

Redefining Profit or Alternatives to the Profit Goal

Vision is replacing profit as the key aim of business. And even profit itself is being redefined in the sense of moving from accounting profit based on short-term expenses internal to the organization to economic profit that considers long-term costs including the organization's effect on society. As O'Toole puts it in *Vanguard Management*, there is

> commitment in word and deed to a higher purpose. These corporations exist to provide society with the goods and services it needs, to provide employment, and to create a surplus of wealth (profit) with which to improve the . . . general standard of living and quality of life. In this view, profit is the means, not the end of corporate activity.

Employee ownership

This issue sits at the core of the shift to the new paradigm, because it relates to individual responsibility, reward, and identity within the organization. It highlights the possibility that the concept of management itself is outmoded in the new paradigm, because the differentiation of workers and managers would be eliminated. In fact, we would drop the term employee from the issue if it weren't for the fact that the meaning of the term would be lost for some. While some people do not want financial ownership, all seem to want an attitude of cooperation within the organization, honoring diversity while establishing community. Surprisingly, when this attitude of equality prevails, a hierarchical structure, often thought to be a symbol of the old paradigm, becomes very useful and new paradigm—an efficiency system rather than a power system.

Creative work

This issue covers everything from the organization of the business to its meaning in society but is centered on the meaning of work for the individual. In one sense this issue is another way of representing what the new paradigm means in business in total. It involves, as consultant Sabina Spencer puts it in a 1989 article in *Organizational Development Practitioner*, people looking for a "deeper sense of life purpose." She continues:

They talk of making a difference, of creating meaningful work, of being fully alive, of living with integrity, of developing sacredness in their relationships, and of turning the organizational environment into a community where everyone can "learn and grow." Meeting bottom line objectives and making sure the "numbers" are right is not enough.

This individual drive for creative work is fueling and is fueled by the move toward transformational organizations with new kinds of purpose, openness, fair and democratic compensation, people being valued with trust and respect, and a thirst for excellence. As the editors of the compendium *Corporate Transformation* assert:

Corporate transformation is a new phenomenon. Never before in the history of the world have so many organizations had to question their very purpose, strategy, structure, and culture. . . . No senior executives of any organization today could or would dispute that one of their major responsibilities is to revitalize their organizations for a competitive world.

Competition, cooperation, cocreation

Some assume that the new paradigm would eliminate aggressive competition completely in a move toward total cooperation or, even better, cocreation. Experience reveals, however, that this is naive, that all three forms of relationship in business are necessary in different situations. Still there is a need for training to determine how to be sensitive to and operate with these three forms.

Community issues

This broad issue ranges from the establishment of community within the organization to the relationship of it to the community in which it resides. For the internal organization, the model of M. Scott Peck in *The Different Drum* provides the best guide to community for business. Peck sees community as inclusive (rather than exclusive) while celebrating diversity. Communication is open and frank, with everyone in the orga-

43

nization being a leader. A community is a safe place where people can make mistakes. When there is conflict, people fight gracefully. A community makes decisions by consensus rather than just democratically. And, in the spirit of being a learning organization, communities contemplate and self-examine. If a business could be a community in Peck's sense, it would also be representing most of the implications of the new paradigm. And it would also be relating to the surrounding community in an integrated instead of an us-versus-them contentious way.

The role of inner wisdom/intuition

Whereas in the past it was thought to be something that only unliberated women had, intuition has become a code word for transformation in business. Yet many fear intuition or don't know how to use it. And intuition used alone can be misleading and have a dark side. But it is clear that intuition and inner wisdom is a key underlying quality of the transformation to the new paradigm. As organizational consultant Roger Harrison writes,

> *Never in my years as a consultant have I seen an organization changed in any fundamental way through rational planning. The leaders I have seen deeply influence their organization's characters and destinies have always operated out of intuition, guided by strongly held purposes and drawn on by a vision of a better future.*

Business as a spiritual discipline/compassion

The gateway from the old paradigm to the new is the individual, and changes in the individual come from the inside, from inner consciousness or spirit. People involved in business transformation have come to it out of their own personal transformation.

Of all of the inner qualities that individuals bring to transformation, compassion plays the most central role. We are not talking here about the mushiness of do-gooders. Instead this compassion leads to one recognizing his or her own inner strength and creativity and also seeing that in others. In business this means that people can have the conflict that is neces-

44

sary for creativity without allowing the conflict to be ad hominem. As in Peck's community, there is fighting with grace. Since compassion includes all of the highest values (honesty, harmony, and integrity), it allows the growth of the new paradigm from the personal to the organizational within business.

The Change in Paradigm

The change in paradigm is driving changes in the form and role of business, and this in turn is leading to transitions in the world. But underlying this is personal change in individuals that leads to changes in organization that leads to business making a new kind of contribution to the world. It is the existence and connection between these two tracks to change (see below) that makes the task of transition to the new paradigm so interesting and complex. But as the authors of *Corporate Transformation* point out, "Actually, any organization that plans to wait for the methods for transformation to be proven effective is probably writing its own epitaph."

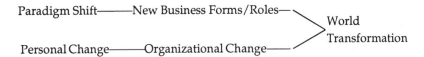

Paradigm Shift————New Business Forms/Roles—\
    World
    Transformation
Personal Change————Organizational Change——/

This suggests that much of the work in this area must be experiential as well as intellectual. While business people need to know in a conceptual sense about the nature of the new paradigm and its roots in science, philosophy, and history, they also need to experience it in terms of their own lives and organizations in order to make these changes operational. Education in the new paradigm will fail if it is entirely old paradigm in nature.

In these times, questions are more important than answers. If we know the right questions, we have something stable to use. We have to continue to ask: What is the nature of the new paradigm? What are the forms and roles of business that would be necessitated by the new paradigm? And given that the shift is occurring, what are the best approaches for making the transition?

HERMAN B. MAYNARD, JR., has more than twenty-one years' experience in professional and line management positions with the Du Pont organization. He is an active participant in the organizational transformation movement, serving as a member of the Board of Governors and treasurer of the World Business Academy, a member of the Transition Board of the National Learning Foundation, a director of People to People International of Delaware, and a Cub Scout den leader.

He has lectured on the new paradigm in business at Stanford University Business School and has delivered speeches to a variety of business and professional organizations. He is coauthor of the monograph *Moving Toward the Millennium: The Corporation in the Twenty-first Century.*

3

The Evolution of Human Consciousness

Herman B. Maynard, Jr.

Accelerating change, uncertainty, paradigm shifts, growth in consciousness—what's happening? What is real? Not real? Are we collectively losing our minds? These questions are being asked by increasing numbers of people, as evidenced by books such as *Global Mind Change* by Willis Harman and *Rapids of Change* by Robert Theobald.

In the spring of 1990, I spent several delightful days with August (Gus) Jaccaci and Mary Baker at their home in the Berkshires, wrestling with questions of paradigm shifts. We challenged ourselves to find a way to articulate what's happening in terms that could be understood by large numbers of people. This chapter describes what emerged after these and many other discussions—a starting point for understanding the evolution of human consciousness.

A New Tool

Gus had developed a tool he called the "metamatrix" with John A. Gowan, a general systems theorist. Studying the evolution of natural systems, Gus and John observed that growth occurs in discrete stages, a fact that had been noted earlier by George Land in his landmark work, *Grow Or Die*. Gus and John postulated four dynamic steps: Gather, Repeat, Share, and Transform. For example, in Figure 1, a particle (Gg), such as an electron or proton, *gathers* in another particle to form an atom (Gr), such as hydrogen or oxygen. This process is *repeated* until a sufficient number of atoms allows combination into a molecule (Gs), such as water, and the molecules then begin to *share* or relate with each other. This process continues until a unique combination of amino acid molecules that we refer to as DNA (Gt) enables *transformation* into a totally different developmental cycle beginning with a living cell (Rg).

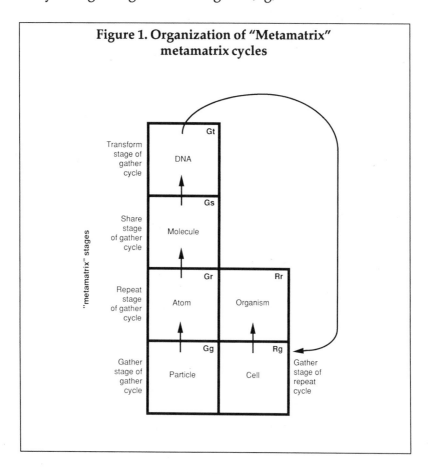

Figure 1. Organization of "Metamatrix"
metamatrix cycles

Just as there are Gather, Repeat, Share, and Transform *stages*, so are there Gather, Repeat, Share, and Transform *cycles*. In the Gathering cycle, the primary activity centers on gathering, while in the Repeat cycle, the activity centers on repeating, and so forth.

Arrayed in metamatrix form, this can be seen as a sixteen-block square with each vertical column or cycle divided into four stages: Gather, Repeat, Share, Transform. Each of the sixteen blocks has what Jaccaci describes as a "distinct creative dynamic." Each block can also be thought of as a paradigm. As one (person, organization, civilization, etc.) moves up the columns, one experiences a paradigm shift between blocks until the process reaches an unstable transformative stage, when a significantly larger paradigm shift or leap takes place to the Gather stage of the next cycle, starting again at the bottom of the next column. To better understand this tool, let's look at the evolution of digital computers in Figure 2.

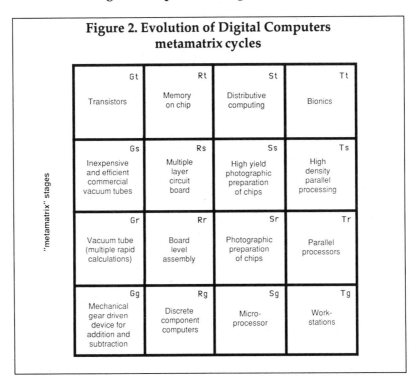

Figure 2. Evolution of Digital Computers metamatrix cycles

"metamatrix" stages

Gt Transistors	Rt Memory on chip	St Distributive computing	Tt Bionics
Gs Inexpensive and efficient commercial vacuum tubes	Rs Multiple layer circuit board	Ss High yield photographic preparation of chips	Ts High density parallel processing
Gr Vacuum tube (multiple rapid calculations)	Rr Board level assembly	Sr Photographic preparation of chips	Tr Parallel processors
Gg Mechanical gear driven device for addition and subtraction	Rg Discrete component computers	Sg Micro-processor	Tg Work-stations

Note that this metamatrix could be seen as one block of the larger subject of "computing," which in turn could be one block of the even larger subject of "communication." In addition, each block of the metamatrix could be subdivided into a sixteen-block grid to yield more detailed insight.

Notice in Figure 2 the embryonic nature of each Gathering stage, such as the discrete component computer (Rg) in the Repeat cycle, which sprang from the invention of the transistor (Gt). This stage was followed by a series of breakthroughs: the assembly of discrete components onto synthetic circuit boards (Rr), the development of multiple layer circuit boards for increased speed and density (Rs), and then the explosive nature of the Transformation stage (Rt), when the etching of chips allowed a manyfold increase in memory capacity, eliminating the need for transistors.

Human Consciousness—A Macro View

Now let's apply the metamatrix concept to the evolution of human consciousness (see Figure 3).

For the purpose of this matrix, the beginning of human consciousness (Gg) is defined as that point when man or woman first experienced separateness. Depending on one's theology or worldview, this separateness can be seen as separate from God or from the universe or from the original causal force. In the physical realm this would manifest as being separate from or at the mercy of one's environment. (If there are berries on the bushes, I eat; if not, I go hungry. If it rains, I get wet; if not, I stay dry.) In psychological terms, at this point the infant begins to distinguish self from others.

For this model, we assume the end point of human consciousness (Tt) is unity, referred to by mystics as the transcendent stage, in which emptiness equals fulfillment. In sensory terms, it is that point at which no value is assigned to hot or cold, wet or dry, satiation or hunger, rich or poor, good or evil. From a more philosophical perspective, this final stage is achieved by mastering the criteria (in the language of Buddhist thinking): "Make no judgment, make no comparison, need no under-

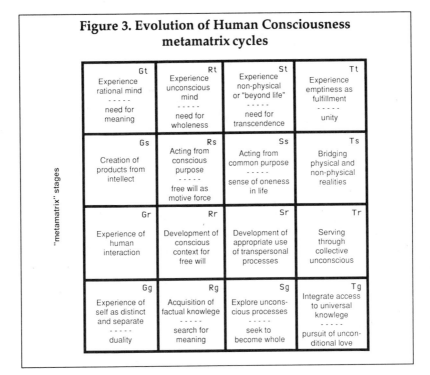

Figure 3. Evolution of Human Consciousness metamatrix cycles

	Gt	Rt	St	Tt
"metamatrix" stages	**Gt** Experience rational mind - - - - - need for meaning	**Rt** Experience unconscious mind - - - - - need for wholeness	**St** Experience non-physical or "beyond life" - - - - - need for transcendence	**Tt** Experience emptiness as fulfillment - - - - - unity
	Gs Creation of products from intellect	**Rs** Acting from conscious purpose - - - - - free will as motive force	**Ss** Acting from common purpose - - - - - sense of oneness in life	**Ts** Bridging physical and non-physical realities
	Gr Experience of human interaction	**Rr** Development of conscious context for free will	**Sr** Development of appropriate use of transpersonal processes	**Tr** Serving through collective unconscious
	Gg Experience of self as distinct and separate - - - - - duality	**Rg** Acquisition of factual knowlege - - - - - search for meaning	**Sg** Explore unconscious processes - - - - - seek to become whole	**Tg** Integrate access to universal knowlege - - - - pursuit of unconditional love

standing." Now let us move ahead momentarily and discuss the Transformation block in each cycle, as this is a point where the movement changes direction and may be less clear.

Presented in Figure 4 are the transformation stages that move us from beginning to end—those experiences that bring to closure one cycle and set the stage for the next. The transformation stage is that point at which everything that has occurred before is necessary but insufficient, creating a tension that propels one forward into a new cycle. In looking at human consciousness or human mind, we can divide these cycles into the development of the physical mind (intellect), conscious mind (rational thought), unconscious mind (intuition), and transcendent mind. We can see that the breakpoint for each transformation step is an experience or awakening to the potential of a greater mind within oneself and the consequent need to pursue this new path.

51

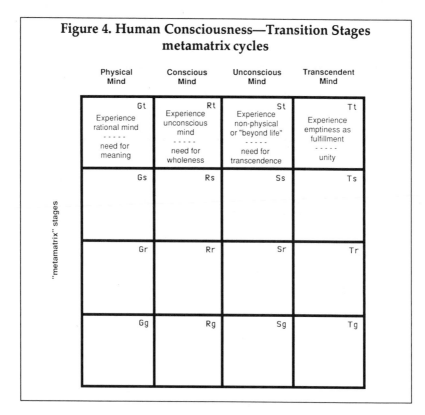

Figure 4. Human Consciousness—Transition Stages
metamatrix cycles

	Physical Mind	Conscious Mind	Unconscious Mind	Transcendent Mind
	Gt Experience rational mind - - - - need for meaning	**Rt** Experience unconscious mind - - - - need for wholeness	**St** Experience non-physical or "beyond life" - - - - need for transcendence	**Tt** Experience emptiness as fulfillment - - - - unity
"metamatrix" stages	Gs	Rs	Ss	Ts
	Gr	Rr	Sr	Tr
	Gg	Rg	Sg	Tg

Early Development

Now let's return to the beginning of the matrix (see Figure 3)—the lower left corner—and follow the development of the vertical column of the Gathering cycle.

The first step in moving from total separateness toward unity is the experience of interaction or relationship with another human being (Gr), leading to primitive family and tribal alignments. Continued evolution leads to the creation of products from intellect (Gs)—putting stones or bushes in front of the cave opening to keep animals away, damming a stream to catch fish, or sharpening a stick for hunting. In this stage there is an intellect but no cognition: all just "is" until one day, man or woman perceives that what "is" could be different. Perceiving that what "is" could be different is reflective of the awakening to rational or conscious thought (Gt). Humankind has now reached the point of thinking about thinking and thus has spawned a hunger for meaning.

Evolution of the human species now shifts from a primary survival orientation to one of acquiring factual knowledge (Rg) and development of the conscious mind. On a societal level, the shift from acquisition of knowledge to development of the concept of free will (Rr) began in the early Egyptian and Chinese cultures about 6000–7000 B.C. and was completed in leading civilizations of the Middle East and Asia by the 5th century B.C. By this time Judaism and Buddhism, as well as the Greek and Egyptian traditions, had adopted a concept of free will that included personal choice—very different from free will as dictated by a king or a god.

The articulation of personal choice as a context for free will (Rr) led directly to the present stage of acting from conscious purpose and the emergence of free will as a motive force (Rs).

The Past 2,500 Years

Let's look at how Western society has evolved into this stage over the past 2,500 years. To help in our discussion, Figure 3, (Rs) "acting from conscious purpose," has been subdivided into a sixteen-block grid or metamatrix, shown in Figure 5.

Personal choice as a context for meaning (Gg) grew in importance among the Essenes and other splinter groups from Judaism from the 5th century B.C. to the advent of John the Baptist and Jesus. Similar development is recorded in the Buddhist traditions. Personal choice as a context for meaning is used here to express the idea that the individual is responsible for developing (or not developing) his or her relationship with God.

In the years after Jesus' appearance, his disciples spread the concepts of personal choice and personal responsibility for achieving salvation (Gr), although this was somewhat modified over the next two centuries to incorporate adherence to church doctrine. Christianity grew throughout the Roman Empire, and in 325 A.D. Emperor Constantine legitimized it (Gs). Unfortunately, the influence of Greco-Roman values on Christian thought declined precipitously when the Vandals and later Goths overthrew the western half of the Roman Empire in the 5th century, resulting in the fall of Rome in 476 A.D. (Gt).

The fall of Rome forced a dramatic shift in consciousness to one of adherence to and refinement of a dogma that governed personal choice—what was appropriate behavior and what was not. With the retrenchment in learning, religious beliefs superseded all other experience (Rg).

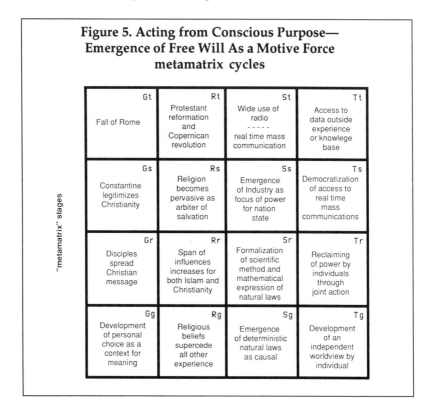

Figure 5. Acting from Conscious Purpose—Emergence of Free Will As a Motive Force metamatrix cycles

"metamatrix" stages

	Gt Fall of Rome	Rt Protestant reformation and Copernican revolution	St Wide use of radio - - - - - real time mass communication	Tt Access to data outside experience or knowlege base
	Gs Constantine legitimizes Christianity	Rs Religion becomes pervasive as arbiter of salvation	Ss Emergence of Industry as focus of power for nation state	Ts Democratization of access to real time mass communications
	Gr Disciples spread Christian message	Rr Span of influences increases for both Islam and Christianity	Sr Formalization of scientific method and mathematical expression of natural laws	Tr Reclaiming of power by individuals through joint action
	Gg Development of personal choice as a context for meaning	Rg Religious beliefs supercede all other experience	Sg Emergence of deterministic natural laws as causal	Tg Development of an independent worldview by individual

By the 7th century, both Islam and Christianity had implemented strict laws governing the actions of believers. High priority was placed on the quest for converts by both religions.

The papacy commissioned teams to convert northern European tribes, while an Islamic Jihad swept the southern crescent of Europe and northern Africa from 632 to 732 A.D., killing all nonbelievers. After 732 A.D., conversion and fidelity to Islam were enforced with a tax on nonbelievers. Through the next few centuries, seven ecumenical councils were held to proscribe what and how a Christian should be and act to achieve spiritual reward. Society was desperately in need of structure, supporting an increase in the span of influence of both Christianity and Islam (Rr).

Strict adherence to a set view of the world eventually led to religion becoming pervasive as the arbiter of a person's salvation (Rs)—an extreme perversion of personal choice as a context for free will. Control of religious thought through temporal means reached its pinnacle with the Inquisition.

The next major transformation occurred with the Protestant Reformation and what we now refer to as the Copernican Revolution (Rt). In the early 16th century, Martin Luther and others espoused the view that each person was responsible for his or her own salvation—a radical split with Church dogma. Strong resistance from Church leaders led to fragmentation of the Church and the formation of numerous sects. In response, a counter-revolution was initiated to stem the erosion of membership.

In the early 17th century, Galileo confirmed the earlier findings of Copernicus that the earth rotated around the sun, effectively showing that from personal observation or from a scientific view (as opposed to contemporary religious thought), the earth was not the center of the universe. This may not have had such a dramatic impact on future events if the Church—where most knowledge resided in the 17th century—had not taken a vigorously opposing stand. A new fracture in the Church had occurred, leading to emergence of a scientific paradigm in a new cycle with the emergence of deterministic natural laws as causal (Sg).

An early and popular champion of this new scientific paradigm and the emergence of natural laws as determined by personal observation was Isaac Newton. Newton saw these natural laws as an expression of the orderliness of God's creation. This scientific paradigm spread rapidly with developments in astronomy, mechanics, mathematics, and other disciplines.

Formalization of scientific methods and the refinement of mathematical expressions of natural laws (Sr) led to the Industrial Age and the emergence of industry as the focus of power and wealth for nation states (Ss). With developments in technology, increasing numbers of people were freed from subsistence-level work. Leisure time to read and participate in the creative arts became more common. Personal choice and personal freedom were becoming rallying cries around the world.

The next major shift occurred with the advent of radio and immediate or real time communication to the masses (St). Through radio, a person anywhere could know almost instantly and continuously what was happening in New York or Paris. Virtually overnight the world had become closer to home and thereby took on increased importance, changing people's worldview.

Development of an independent worldview (Tg) set the stage for reclaiming of power of individuals through joint action (Tr), perhaps most obviously evidenced in the United States by the civil rights movement in the 1960s, as well as the women's movement, the Vietnam anti-war movement, anti-nuclear arms movement, and so on. Personal development was popularized with "T" groups, est, and motivation seminars.

In the 1980s, in a new Information Age, low-cost personal computers and computer networking rapidly evolved to provide a framework in which literally any individual with the desire could communicate directly with very large numbers of people around the world (Ts). With this real time communication, a platform was created for synchronous action on agreed-upon causes. Peoples of the world could, in concert, respond to each other's needs and, if they chose, could withdraw their support. People now had a vehicle to take back their power from a government or an institution.

As we enter the 1990s, another shift is well under way, which I describe as having access to data outside of one's experience or knowledge base (Tt). Whether triggered by a dream or flash of intuitive insight, more and more individuals are opening to a belief that they are more than their physical body and that somewhere within themselves is a source of wisdom and compassion greater than they have known before. And somehow, in some way, a belief is emerging that at some level within we are all connected to each other. We are truly one. With this belief everything that has occurred before in the development of our material world is insufficient. This material world brought us to where we are, but is no longer sufficient to carry us further without something more. This need for more, this need for wholeness, propels us into and through the transformation block "experiencing the unconscious mind," which will in turn propel us into the next Gather stage.

What's Ahead?

Figure 6 represents a subdivision of the Transformation block, titled Experience Unconscious Mind—Need for Wholeness, shown in Figure 3 (Rt). It represents the paradigm many believe lies just ahead of us.

Developed from the common experiences of individuals awakening to the unconscious mind, it provides a model for helping us understand where we are and where we are headed.

Although a few individuals have evolved to higher levels of consciousness up to and including unity, Western society as a whole is just now approaching the halfway point. The paradigm shift under way now is moving into the Transformation stage of the Repeat cycle (Figure 3, Rt) of human consciousness and portends to be as significant for the human species as the shift that occurred with the initial experience of the rational or conscious mind by primitive men and women.

Analyses of other transitions using the metamatrix as described in the preceding pages indicate that we will be propelled through time with a force much stronger than the one that pushed us through the Information Age or the Industrial Age or the Copernican Revolution.

Figure 6. Experience Unconscious Mind—Need for Wholeness metamatrix cycles

	Gt	Rt	St	Tt
	Hypothesis of different reality	Redefinition of reality - - - - - "I know the answers"	Disenchantment and realization of complexity - - - - - "I really don't have the answers"	Wonderment - - - - - "I really don't have the answer and I choose to seek"
	Gs	**Rs**	**Ss**	**Ts**
	Discussion in protected space	Form a support group	Outreach through public channels	Witness mode - - - - - conversation of ego with higher self
	Gr	**Rr**	**Sr**	**Tr**
	Identify parallels in outer world	Experiment with new forms of intuitive processes	Form or join an organization as a platform to grow	Confront paradox of wholeness of self and oneness with all
	Gg	**Rg**	**Sg**	**Tg**
	Seek data outside of experience or knowlege base	Seek new experiences and information to define the field	Seek converts	Seek understanding of depth and diversity of intuitive processes

("metamatrix" stages along left vertical axis)

The evolution of human consciousness into and beyond the cycle of discovering the conscious mind as represented in Figure 3 and Figure 4 will bring the spiritual development of the human species to a level and intensity that parallels the drive for material success held as a worldview for the past 8,000 years. Can we now conceive of this new worldview?

Implications

Much of what I have presented here may be applicable only to the Western industrialized world and needs to be reconceptualized for the technologically underdeveloped and developing civilizations. Some of these cultures, such as the Aborigines in the Australian outback, are likely to be ahead of

58

the Western world in development of the unconscious mind, while others are likely to be behind us.

In addition, within the industrialized West, there is great disparity in levels of development. The biggest question in my mind is how we as a world—all people of the world—can navigate the passage ahead without causing disfranchisement or alienation of those less ready for opening to the unconscious mind. If we are to avoid unnecessary and destructive conflict, we must accept people as they choose to be instead of expecting them to conform to our worldview.

JIM CHANNON is co-owner of Balian Design Studios and works with his wife and partner Joan. They perform strategic design consulting with executives in their studios in Hawi, Hawaii. They specialize in weaving matters of spirit into organizational life.

Mr. Channon was the lead futurist for the U.S. Army, where he designed a high-tech light infantry division, a training center for the 21st century, and a military culture for the future called "The First Earth Battalion." He is the creator of Advanced Visual Language and the strategic design process where his high-speed graphic illustrations capture corporate thinking in ways that communicate powerfully to the work force. He is a fellow of the World Business Academy.

4

Esprit de Corps

Jim Channon

People don't so much want to know the meaning of life as they want to have an "experience" of it.
—Joseph Campbell

There is that poignant point in time when a manager graduates to become the boss. When this happens, the new CEO is thrust into the leadership posture as the tribal elder of the enterprise. The soul and the spirit of the organization are now his or her special responsibility. I would like to suggest that knowing the meaning of the corporation's purpose in the world and having a tangible "experience" of that purpose constitute *esprit de corps* for the employees. Esprit de corps is a sense of ownership in the corporate enterprise that is generated by an experience I will hereafter refer to as *spirit*.

When people had tribes to go home to, or villages where they could share the seasonal festival, or even neighborhoods with some personal intimacy, these more spirit-evoking elements of culture were part of the natural order of life. But, as we approach the 21st century, our business cultures have become our "tribes"—our villages and neighborhoods. They are the building blocks that will shape our planetary culture. Our older social cultures have become atomized by communications technology and commuting and have largely disappeared as a consequence. So, if there is no experience of spirit in corporations, then there may not be much spirit in the civilization at large.

CEOs no longer have the wizards, muses, storytellers, witch doctors, and other "spiritual assistants" once afforded the chiefs and leaders of cultures with sizable populations. Rather, modern leaders have been trained to focus on the fine art of making things, not the cultural art of evoking spirit. Historically, leaders have sought support for a variety of invocations, dedications, blessings, and occasionally prayers.

It is not "management doctrine" that dictates we build a rich culture of spirit and experience in our corporate lives—it's just common sense! Loyalty is a two-way street. Leadership provides a total cultural experience and the work force should provide loyalty, energy, and dedicated service. As George Bernard Shaw says, "I am of the opinion that my life belongs to the whole community. And as long as I live it is my privilege, my privilege to do for it whatever I can. . . . Life is no brief candle. To me it is a sort of splendid torch which I've got to hold up for the moment and I want to make it burn as brightly as possible before handing it on to future generations." What would it take to have the average employee look at his life with the company with this kind of passion?

Author and poet Robert Bly says, "Corporations do so much to produce the sanitized, hairless, shallow man." That, of course, is simply a matter of choice and one that I have found unacceptable to many leaders presently at work in the world. It doesn't mean, however, that those leaders have had access to a robust set of tools on how to handle spirit in the corporation. They have not.

Tribal Council

Dialogue "Round the Fire"

How natural it is to share stories around the camp fire. Why have we allowed such a genuinely rich experience to be relegated to kids at camp? Perhaps, because it doesn't go with our modern office air conditioning or "open office" furniture systems? The really sad news is that most people now consider meetings, usually held in windowless, stagnant conference rooms, as one of the least productive events on the corporate menu.

The noted physicist, David Bohm, has recently elaborated on the concept of "dialogue" wherein he highlights the value of talking together without a specific purpose in order to calibrate and leaven the group for a greater cooperation later. Full expression clears the deck for action. The philosopher Martin Buber says, "But where the dialogue is fulfilled in its being, between partners who have turned to one another in truth, who express themselves without reserve, there is brought into being a memorable common *fruitfulness* which is to be found nowhere else."

Native Americans and other tribal groups still practice some form of council. This is also a standard tool being used by the fast growing men's movement in America. The process is not good for making decisions about the viability of one business strategy versus another, and it won't replace all other meetings. But, periodically, this style of intimate exchange contributes spirit to the growth of the organization and the people in it.

In the typical corporate meeting context, several important features of the tribal council process have been forgotten:

An equal chance for each participant to set the tone/context
The allowance of emotional, spiritual, and cultural offerings
Full disclosure of the truth without retribution

We often forget that the first person to speak in a meeting can capture the direction of the meeting, since we Westerners are habituated to following the agenda or thrust of the subject.

This is in contrast to the consensus style of the East, wherein content is not as important as hearing each participant, even if they repeat the same idea others have said previously.

In tribal council, we can learn from the Orient as well as our U.S. native forebears. As the talking stick is passed around the circle, each person may offer a totally unique comment. On the second round of the circle, individuals can build on any of the previous comments or issues raised. The individuals therefore reach a consensus as to where the focus should reside, whether in one area or many. The depth of the feelings can mix freely with the clarity of the thinking.

In council, the connection between work at hand, matters of spirit, emotional issues, or ideas involving the cultural well-being of the organization are integrated and discussed. These are matters that flavor a rich culture and unfortunately are not included in many present-day agenda-driven meetings. The possibility of speaking about spiritual connections in an organizational forum also means that the mystery and wonder of life aren't excluded from daily existence.

The council circle is a very common formation for corporate trainings done to examine values and renew vision. Something "personal" occurs in a circular array, especially once the tables are removed. Physical obstacles seem to act as barriers to the exchange of human energy. Driving through Tokyo at night, one sees office after office of employees gathered tightly around small desks working through the details of a project together. In contrast, office workers in high tech companies are separated by cubicles and soundproof barriers. I notice the "work-energy" increases with physical closeness and when the circle is round in shape, more like a container. For instance, in pre- and post-game "huddles," football players naturally embrace and often pray together. The formation makes a difference to them and the spirit they experience.

Corporate leaders from AT&T, Du Pont, Kodak, and other major Fortune 100 firms have engaged in circles of "truth-telling" at Larry Wilson's Pecos River Conference Center. Larry's clients get down "to the bones" quickly this way. It seems less threatening to pursue "sticky" issues at work, as well as personal obstacles to performance, after a great couple of days of teamwork and courage building on his ropes course. Revealing difficult information requires team support and courage. Chris Majer and a company called SPORTSMIND in Seattle specialize in core skills training including, honesty, integrity, and accountability.

I can imagine a fire pit being part of the 21st century corporate office, so that the council process would have an authentic place to occur. I imagine the CEO as tribal elder, guiding the intimate evolution of his or her people. Remember, there may not be any cultural grouping other than the corporation in the future for transformation. I anticipate that the competitive, full-culture corporations of the 21st century will strive to contribute to this more intimate side of the human experience.

The Technology: Here and throughout this chapter I want to speculate about the operative principles that make examples like sitting together in circle function effectively in the corporation.

People create a field of energy about them. When those fields of energy merge, the "collective field" becomes more unified and stronger. To have an experience or felt sense of being together, the circular formation acts as a container and amplifier of those collective energy fields.

65

If you want to bond a group or allow natural human energy to boost a team's productivity, be sensitive to the shape of the container, at your meetings and in the office itself.

Vision

The Organization's Higher Purpose

Belonging to a group, especially a group that is making a difference in the world, can be a powerful motivating factor. People who know they are working for something larger with a more noble purpose can be expected to be loyal and dependable and, at a minimum, more inspired.

It is painfully obvious that people who sense there is more to life than work would like it if their broader aspirations and sense of service wouldn't have to be left out of their corporate life. I find that corporations today are very open to making a contribution to society or the world at large. The problem remains that once involved in formulas of productivity and bottom-line results, few leaders have any practical experience in translating spiritual interests into the corporate workplace. Again, there is a classic shortage of management-based tools to integrate values-based thinking into corporate work life. The muse is absent.

"Visioning" has been a fairly common element on the corporate training docket and conference agenda. It is the classically distinct responsibility of the CEO or president, but is now often developed in concert with the leadership team.

All too often, accustomed to bottom-line management, the new CEO will simply write a composite "vision statement" built around obvious corporate goals. Other common approaches include an assembly of current corporate buzz words: *excellence, quality, performance,* etc. Some product-oriented leaders can't understand the value of creating anything beyond a "mission statement." The Industrial Age mentality is still at work here and is organized around production. The thought of "contribution" or "service" to the larger system and how to manage it is more obscure.

Recently, corporations like Chase Manhattan Bank, Du Pont, AT&T, Apple Computer, and others have tackled the subject of "contribution" by including a new question in their search for a vision: What is our higher purpose?

When this question is posed to working groups at conferences, they usually discuss goals, missions, and strategies until the subject of "service" comes up. At this point the energy in the room usually shifts. It is worthwhile to notice the subtle but expanded feeling in the "field." People seem visibly inspired to adventure into the area of *higher service*. Higher service generally means service to humanity, the world, or the environment. In this way, the individual's inner quest to have some "purpose" in life becomes integrated with the corporate purpose and vision.

The Du Pont agricultural products team (makers of herbicides) responded to the question of higher purpose by creating a vision topped by a banner headline: "A NEW PARTNERSHIP WITH NATURE ." Now this kind of higher purpose can bring forth within a culture a commitment that transcends scheduled work hours. It can offer a deeper meaning and sense of right livelihood to people in a world where the noblest expression of interest has been limited to such corporate platitudes as, "Increase the market share by twenty-five percent in the next five years." The individual's sense of purpose, meaning, and alignment with the corporate purpose increase the esprit de corps in an organization.

General Electric says, "We bring good things to life." Sluglines at the bottom of corporate advertising tell us that businesses as cultural players at least intend a better world for us all. Every little good intention helps.

> *The Technology: It has been known for centuries that positive thinking produces positive results. To think something has an effect on becoming that thing. If a tribal elder fails to encourage high option thinking, then high option results may not be realized. The profound simplicity in asking the question, "What is our higher purpose?" on a recurring basis seems an entirely healthy process, which*

will probably induce several positive self-fulfilling prophecies. At the very minimum, if you don't have a slugline under your corporate logo, ask your core team or entire company to engage in a contest to create one. Often a companion training process can be to review values and vision. Notice the collection of associated topics included in the corporate vision illustration below.

In an integrated strategic design or complete corporate vision, the higher purpose pulls the work force while the mission, goals, and objectives tend to do the pushing.

Communion

Rites of Passage

Corporations are often born from small companies that grow incrementally over time. The folklore that generates during that time constitutes its tradition. Tradition and folklore define a culture over time and give the work force a sense that they belong to something that is publicly recognized as valuable. Yet, today, corporations can be born overnight, by growing up around a product or through a corporate restructuring. The result is that we have many large new cultures being created that have *mass* but no "experience," or tradition, and no bonding as a group. They produce people who feel like technical components in a production machine but have little sense of tribe, or blood, or community.

The rite of passage or common challenge has been used historically to bond groups of people and bring them into the fold. Recently, corporations have successfully employed the outdoor challenge events, or "Ropes Courses" as they are called, to recreate a powerful common adventure experience for people. The adventure may be totally irrelevant to corporate performance skills, but if people experience a physical and spirit-filled team challenge, they can easily bond in their common passage through this challenge and take that deeper connection back to the office.

Soldiers have always considered basic training to be full of irrelevant "chickenshit" requirements. Yet, basic training brings people together who have no past history and bonds them in a series of common challenges that cause them to reveal themselves, laugh at their vulnerability, and recognize that no matter how challenging the task, if they pull together they can succeed. They are getting a chance to "scrimmage" together without risk. During the days of the volunteer army the U.S. Army eliminated the chickenshit and focused on the skills training alone. When they found out that the troops had nothing to overcome or brag about, they reinstituted the older pressure-cooker style.

69

The Army in particular must make very tough physical demands upon its employees. So they extend the rites of passage in basic training to the extreme. But, once the common challenge has been mastered, the rewards are heaped on. The candidates are awarded the insignia of the units they join; they wear badges that reflect their proficiency with weapons, equipment, or skills; they march together as a group to the grand sound of a military band; they resume normal sleeping and leave privileges; and they are permitted to participate in the harassment of the next group of candidates. They are made to believe in dozens of small ways that they "belong" and that they've "earned that right."

I recognize that bonding in this extreme way is appropriate for groups who must face danger together and not so appropriate for a bay of technical workers. But, it would be a mistake, culturally, to overlook this entire phenomenon as being "old fashioned" and deny employees the chance to feel a special connection to each other by way of a challenging experience.

The Technology: Rites of Passage are not a rational activity. They are designed to bring physical and emotional energy to a climax, bonding a group. They produce an "experience," not an "ah-ha!" Corporations have produced ropes course events to provide a physical challenge. Some groups have also included an emotional challenge of revealing deep fears and significant life-changing events. The key here is that all candidates are on trial and are made to believe their ordeal together is really tough. Whatever the "ordeal," it should make good story-telling material. The physical events produce courage as a by-product and an abiding sense that as a team anything can be accomplished. *The emotional events remind participants of affection, honesty, and the feeling of belonging to a family. The combined result can be an organization unafraid to face new challenges together and able to communicate honestly about things that are not working.*

The rites of passage are brought to a peak with a graduation ceremony that includes the presentation of common rewards to identify achievement and belonging.

Celebration

Corporate Cathedral

Watching major corporations produce their "big" shows to honor sales stars or introduce new product lines is a unique peek at a modern day extravaganza! There are door prizes and famous personalities and often Disney-like themes with costumes and music to boot. The corporation is looking to create a meaningful "experience" for a larger group than the council group, and may hope to motivate a hundred or a thousand or more people.

Recently, some of these extravaganzas have included aspects of spirit and transformation. For example, the openings of the Olympic Games and the Goodwill Games are very colorful, enthusiastic, and have all the aspects of a "big" show. The observable difference here is that these extravaganzas are a re-dedication to a set of principles, like sportsmanship and international goodwill. As such, they are exemplary of older traditions like those found in cathedrals wherein the psyche is overlaid with color, splendor, and music, all designed to reinforce a set of values and beliefs. Kathy deForrest has some interesting elaboration on this kind of conscious celebration in *Transforming Work*, a book edited by John Adams.

General Motors of Canada recently introduced their new vision and reworked values with an interesting form of "Corporate Cathedral." Each of the manufacturing units was asked to "build" a small float representing one of the values to be reinforced. These floats were used to kick off a day-long event inside the convention hall of a large Toronto hotel. The floats paraded around to the color commentary of television-style hosts as they circled the convention hall to the rousing music of a local Army band. The president, CEO, and his staff, in their shirt sleeves, then took their places in a half circle on the center stage. The other half circle was filled by the audience of 650 manufacturing representatives. A large full-color painting of the group vision was unveiled. The CEO, using the painting, took to a wonderful old-style kind of story telling to unveil the details of their projected future. The primary theme was "Customers for life," which was enabled and graphically depicted by an entire range of very principled actions. Using the motto " I am GM," which underpinned the entire painting, the employees were invited to see themselves as being responsible, at any moment, for the company as well as its products and services.

Following the CEO, the youngest and the oldest members of the team made presentations. This was yet another example of the cultural richness that was evoked. The day ended with a young international singing and dancing group called Up With People. One hundred strong, they sang the GM Acceleration

Song that had been rewritten to include the new values and vision elements created by the leadership team.

The consistent component of this General Motors extravaganza was that each element of the production was designed to reinforce a building block of the organization's future as a culture. It was intentionally focused on meaningful ideas and brought to the level of an "experience" by overlaying the senses with artistry.

Whirlpool Corporation recently acquired Dutch, German, and Italian appliance companies. The CEO recognized that the vision that inspired the company must now be a global one. He chose a hotel in Montreux, Switzerland, that was neutral territory for the newly acquired European cultures and employed a wide variety of transformational tools to bond this new international consortium into *one global company.*

For example, to honor each of the contributions made by the sixteen nations involved, a world-class multimedia presentation was prepared for each country where Whirlpool now had interests. The presentations included a first-class piece on the *global vision* developed by the leadership team. The staging of these presentations was impeccable, with lighting, sound, and music created by a large artistic team from England. The corporate logo was transformed into two large gold crests placed prominently on stages left and right.

The effect again was to produce an "experience" of *quality* for ideas that were important to this budding new culture at a very deep level. This was, as the Germans said, a new Whirlpool Corporate Code.

The Technology: I am afraid it's all too common for corporations to assemble themselves in large auditoriums and hear the boss monotone a short message of significance from behind a wooden podium. If an idea is important intellectually, it should be presented spiritually and emotionally if inspired action is to result. People will ascribe importance to ideas that the corporate leadership signals are important. Large gatherings can be far more than an "experience" of fun. If the content is pertinent to the operating code and future direction of the corporate culture, however, then the treatment is more empowered by having the culturally significant ideas delivered in an artistically rich and refined environment. In the corporate setting spirit is like fuel—if it is rich enough, the work force produces far beyond the expected work day. An inspired collective sense of purpose is as much an energy event as an information event. Think energy.

If an effort or the presentation of the corporate vision is meant to be important, then each should be credentialed with an event approaching corporate cathedral.

The challenge for business leaders in the 21st century is to assume the mantle of spiritual elder for their cultures, so that life doesn't become trivial and gray for all the people who spend most of their life at work. Corporations *are* our new communities. Let's enjoy them.

WILLIAM C. MILLER is co-founder and principal consultant for California-based Global Creativity Corporation. He is the author of *The Creative Edge: Fostering Innovation Where You Work* and *Creativity: The Eight Master Keys* (an audio program that is the first training package recommended by *Fortune* magazine). In the 1980s, he was senior management consultant for the innovation management program at SRI International. In the late 1970s, he was corporate manager of training and development for Victor Equipment Company. His clients now include Hewlett-Packard, Compaq, Levi Strauss, Procter & Gamble, Pillsbury, and Du Pont.

Mr. Miller's seminar materials on innovation have been licensed by the Wilson Learning Corporation for worldwide development and distribution. He has delivered seminars and keynotes on innovative management practices in countries such as Japan, Singapore, Czechoslovakia, Bulgaria, Holland, Canada, and the United States.

5

How Do We Put Our Spiritual Values to Work?

William C. Miller

"Living the Question"

A few years ago, the Corporate Innovation Committee at the 3M Corporation invited me to make a presentation on strategic innovation management. At the time, I was in charge of the Innovation Management Program at SRI (Stanford Research Institute) International, an international think tank and consulting firm. At the end of the presentation, the 3M manager who brought me in saw a book in my briefcase as I was packing. It had a faded gold cross on it.

"What are you reading, William?" he asked.

"Oh, it's a book about six saints from the 13th to 16th centuries."

That's all I planned to say, being shy to talk about spiritual things with my clients.

"What prompts your interest in that—religious conviction, curiosity, philosophy?"

"Well, to tell the truth, for a few years now I've realized that a major theme in my life and work has been *'How might spirituality, creativity, and business somehow be facets of the same diamond rather than separate subjects?'"*

He responded, "That's amazing. That's exactly what's been on my mind the past six months! Let's get a bite to eat and talk about that."

And so we did. We discussed how spirituality was more than the differing beliefs and practices of organized religions ... how creativity encompassed how we expressed our unique individuality as well as how we responded to work challenges ... how business included any organization involved in an "exchange of value," whether they be profit enterprises, government, education, or nonprofit institutions. We discussed how we all share in an "original wound" (of the heart) that builds walls between these fundamental parts of our lives and psyches.

As we sensed a kinship and a longing to talk with others about how to heal this "original wound" through our work, the question shifted to: *"How do we put our spiritual values to work?"*

Those two questions, "How might spirituality, creativity, and business somehow be facets of the same diamond?" and "How do we put our spiritual values to work?" are *living questions* for me. They're about the nature of living, and they've taken on their own lives within me, providing insights and "answers-for-now" that continually evolve and get richer.

In fact, *living with the question* has been rich to the extent that I don't settle for any single answer, as if the finality of a conclusion would kill the living process within me. Like nature, the question recycles itself as part of my own revitalization.

Spiritual Values

Many years ago, I made a pilgrimage to India, hoping to find a way to renew my spiritual life, even to revitalize the core values of my Christian heritage. Sitting in an auditorium with thousands of people listening to a teacher named Sathya Sai

Baba, I heard words that cracked a hard shell around my heart. In paraphrase he said, "Realize that Divinity resides at the deepest core of your being. The deeper you go within, the closer you come to that Divine center."

Walking out of the auditorium, I was stunned. For so long, I believed that the deeper I went into my own nature—as an Original Sinner of no worth—the *further* I would get from God. His words felt true, as if they came from a long-hidden voice of inner conscience. Perhaps for the first time in my life, I breathed a sigh of real inner peace.

Thus, I began a path of discovering how the spiritual side of ourselves (that naturally exists within us) and spiritual values might naturally emerge in us as they did in the great founders of the world's religions: Jesus, Moses, Buddha, Zoroaster, Mohammed, Krishna. How did their own lives speak their true message? What did they stand for—literally?

We may use different words, but the core values are always there: *inner peace, truth, right-conduct, nonviolence (which I like to call "well-being"),* and, above all, *love.* (When asked which was the greatest commandment, didn't Christ say, "Love" ?)

Quite often, the religious institutions that followed these founders did not live up to their examples. For example, how can Protestants and Catholics kill each other in the name of the same Jesus Christ who lived and breathed love?

Yet all of these values—peace, truth, right-action, well-being, and love—have their source in the Divinity that is at our deepest core. The great founders are our examples of the pinnacle of the human merging with the Divine, and they taught that love is an integral part of our being. Putting spiritual values to work can be something that is innately *natural* to us, rather than needing imposed rules.

I trust that there is a natural wisdom hidden by our mistakes, our errors, our "sins." When we're honest with ourselves, we can learn what brings us closer to our spiritual nature and what doesn't. Living with peace, truth, right-action, well-being, and love can become quite natural.

The goal of living as Christ, or Buddha, or the other founders lived is to find our way home to the experience of living—and working—according to these values, such as *truth*.

The "Practical" Side of Spiritual Values

In 1987, Frank Carrubba became the Director of the Hewlett-Packard Laboratory, which conducts all the centralized research and development for this key player in the global electronics industries. Frank conducted a study at the HP labs to find out what the difference was between research teams that did not achieve their goals, teams that did accomplish them, and teams that were extremely successful and consistently far exceeded their goals. His study concluded:

> *If you looked at those that were truly successful, those that really stood out above and beyond the other teams, we found that those teams had leaders and managers (sometimes the same person and sometimes not) who treated their customers as they themselves wanted to be treated . . . that they found in themselves qualities and spirit and truth and they brought it out in their customers. They were people who had no reason to wear a particular mask, because they were always what they were every single hour of the day.*
>
> *So successful teams . . . had a relationship with their customer that was a personal relationship, one that allowed people to be all they could be and not worry about struggling day after day trying to represent themselves as being something that they weren't. And that was really special among those people, and it came out clearly.*

"They found in themselves qualities and spirit and truth and they brought it out in their customers. . . . (They) had a relationship with their customer that was a personal relationship, one that allowed people to be all they could be and not worry about struggling day after day trying to represent themselves as being something that they weren't. . . ."

When I first heard him report these extraordinary conclusions, I was amazed and yet not amazed. I was surprised to hear it brought out so clearly. Yet, after all, it made perfect sense to me that personal authenticity, caring, and truthfulness would open up a level of communication, and communion, in which extraordinary work could flourish.

Another example of applying spiritual values to work comes from Dick Eppel, then general manager of a communication systems division of a major electronics corporation. He took that job with the assignment of turning the division around. He reports:

> It was definitely a division in serious trouble, a result of too much success in their marketing activities without enough forethought given to how they were going to execute that success. Clearly one goal had to be to satisfy the customer. And the second thing was to get the people to believe that there was a recovery possible here.

> And so we set up a prioritization of what customers we were going to satisfy when, with the goal in mind that we were going to satisfy all customers. We would not take on any more business whatsoever that would jeopardize satisfying our current customers.

> Everything had to be credible in the sense that the road map, the vision, the how-you're-going-to-get-there all had to be credible. I was the one who had to say, "No." I was the one who had to say, "Trust me." I was the one who had to say, "Once we get through this, then we are all going to win."

One time, a salesman came to Dick with a potential new customer who wanted a delivery date that he knew they couldn't meet. The salesman wanted an exception to their strategy so he could get the sale. He told me:

> I hung tough on not accepting business that we couldn't deliver on. That was a test. I would talk to a customer, look him in the eye, and say, "Do you want me to lie to you?" I used words that had an emotional impact, but there was no ambiguity. They accepted that. It turned out that we could execute good business, deliver on that business, and manage it to a schedule, even though there were threats of going someplace else or walking away from it.

*After two years things were significantly improved. Turn-
over was down. We got the division to break even, or pretty
close to break even. Every contract got delivered on. Every
contract. The most important piece that we saved has
represented about $13-20 million per year of cash-rich
profits ever since.*

What did it take for Dick and his division to succeed? He
named two primary factors beyond having the right strategy:

*One was a sense of positivity and perseverance: positive
expectations, positive visualization. The second thing that
was going on was that the management team, for one
reason or another, amalgamated in a way that was very
unique to me. I've always enjoyed working with people,
always felt like I had good teams to work with, and the
friendship and comradery was there. But in this operation
there was one other level that was a bonding beyond
friendship and comradery. There was just a sense of caring
and a sense of concern. And I even use the words of "a
genuine sense of love" between the parties, even though
that was never expressed verbally.*

Truth telling. Love. Business. They need each other—truth
and love enrich business success, and business is a way for love
to express itself fully and openly, serving people's needs.

Spiritual Values and Economic Reality

Along with so many others, I was thrilled by the momen-
tous changes of the late 1980s in the Soviet Union and Eastern
Europe. I was also thrilled by Gorbachev's visit to the Pope.
Reporters asked Gorbachev if the visit meant that churches in
the Soviet Union would be more open. His affirmative reply
made headlines.

Yet something else he said was even more noteworthy to
me. He added that unless the types of personal values taught by
the spiritual traditions were revived in the Soviet people, they
would not succeed in rebuilding the economy! Perhaps we in
the West have such a hard time associating spiritual values and
business, we didn't believe that was the real news.

82

But then, even in the Soviet Union, such a topic was new. During my trip to Moscow in 1988, some of my best conversations with people were on the question, "With all the turmoil and changes, what deep cultural values can the Soviet people call upon to stabilize their feelings and their choices? What can keep them from being swept up into the free-enterprise opportunity for greed and special interests?"

Those questions were often met with silence at first—as if they were ideas that were brand new, or perhaps old and dusty from disuse. But invariably, delight and soberness followed in thoughtful dialogue. One person who had been to the West quite often said, "In Russia, when someone asks, 'How are you?' they mean it. They'll stop for as long as it takes to really hear how you are. This is not so very much in the West, I find. This sincere caring is something we need to tap into."

Later, Vaclav Havel said in his inaugural address as President of Czechoslovakia, "We have been lied to a great deal, and I don't presume you elected me to lie to you more. We are a morally ill country." He went on to say that unless the people of Czechoslovakia learned to be truthful, open, and respectful with each other, they would never succeed in rebuilding the economy and country.

This was an extension of what Havel wrote in the late 1970s:

> If a better economic and political model is to be created, then perhaps more than ever before it must derive from profound existential and moral changes in society. This is not something that can be designed and introduced like a new car. If it is to be more than just a new variation on the old degeneration, it must above all be an expression of life in the process of transforming itself. A better system will not automatically ensure a better life. In fact, the opposite is now true: only by creating a better life can a better system be developed.

We in the West are in the same boat. It's just easier to see in the black-and-white need for renewal of the Eastern European countries. We face the same need, the same calling. Our powers to affect the environment and the well-being of people all over the planet make this spiritual renewal absolutely critical to our economic and social health.

We've been playing in the stagnant airs of inquiry about what produces innovation and business growth. How can we lift ourselves up and breathe in fresh insight, to "in-spire" our businesses and societies in this age of economic and social transformation?

In October 1990, I gave a speech at a large gathering of managers and consultants from Eastern and Western Europe on "Strategic Management and Innovation." The conference, in Prague, Czechoslovakia, had been planned since 1988, well before the events of 1989 in Eastern Europe made this gathering auspiciously well-timed. As I listened to other speakers, two messages struck me deeply.

The first was from Alan Mintzberg, a professor of management at McGill University in Canada. He echoed words I'd first heard from Willis Harman twenty years ago, but they were in a new context. He said that the events in Eastern Europe in 1989 demonstrated to everyone that centrally planned economies don't work: they don't foster initiative, innovation, or productivity. However, he added that when we look at many prime examples of "free enterprise giants," they've actually functioned as centrally planned economies operating as a corporation (instead of country)—and that they don't foster initiative, innovation, or productivity either! That's why these long-established "giants" are becoming less competitive in the global market.

His caution to the Eastern Europeans was sobering: as they import Western management practices, "watch out for what you import." Many practices may seem familiar, and that's a big problem for both sides.

The second message that stayed with me was from Professor Stanislav Adamec, advisor to Havel, who spoke of the need to "improve the spiritual potential of thinking, working, and overall lifestyle . . . to lead people to the courage they need to excel and to work deliberately and purposefully."

He added that "the absence of truth about the conditions of life is a direct threat to economic and social development" and that "confidence and trust were important to build a world without frontiers of violence."

This emphasis on spiritual potential, on truthfulness, trust, and respect points to the core values that have been taught by the holy books throughout the ages. As Gorbachev said, unless we revitalize these values in ourselves and others, we cannot prosper in the years ahead. And perhaps the lack of those values is what has generated the "centrally planned, centrally controlled" mentality we have employed, whether in Eastern Europe, Western corporations, or anywhere.

An appreciation of deep, cultural values and a conscious development of those values is essential to any healthy business growth. At their very deepest, these cultural values usually reflect the core values of the region's spiritual traditions.

How we put our spiritual values to work can make a huge difference to our own quality of life, and that also is the foundation for each organization in our society to become prosperous, successful, and healthy.

That certainly was the message from Frank Carrubba, and Dick Eppel as well. And it leads me to conclude with a slight evolution to the "living question" of this chapter:

"How well do we put our spiritual values to work?"

Part II

Recognizing the larger context and the potential constructive role of business in a global transformation, the following chapters examine key elements and strategies that will enable visionary business men and women to embody these new traditions.

PETER M. SENGE, Ph.D., directs the Systems Thinking and Organizational Learning Program at the Sloan School of Management at the Massachusetts Institute of Technology. He is a founding partner of Innovation Associates, a management consulting firm based in the Boston area dedicated to supporting the creation of high performing organizations. Dr. Senge is one of the creators of the Innovation Associates' Leadership & Mastery program.

This chapter contains excerpts from an article previously published by *Sloan Management Review* and is reprinted with permission of the publisher.

Dr. Senge's work on leadership in complex systems grows out of his training in systems engineering, social systems modeling, and human consciousness. In late 1990, his bestselling book *The Fifth Discipline: The Art and Practice of the Learning Organization* was published by Doubleday. He has degrees from Stanford University and MIT. He has lectured widely throughout the United States and Canada.

6

The Leader's New Work:
Building Learning Organizations

Peter M. Senge

Human beings are designed for learning. No one has to teach an infant to walk, or talk, or master the spatial relationships needed to stack eight building blocks that don't topple. Children come fully equipped with an insatiable drive to explore and experiment. Unfortunately, the primary institutions of our society are oriented predominantly toward controlling rather than learning, rewarding individuals for performing for others rather than for cultivating their natural curiosity and impulse to learn. The young child entering school discovers quickly that the name of the game is getting the right answer and avoiding mistakes—a mandate no less compelling to the aspiring manager.

"Our prevailing system of management has destroyed our people," writes W. Edwards Deming, leader in the quality movement. "People are born with intrinsic motivation, self-esteem, dignity, curiosity to learn, joy in learning. The forces of destruction begin with toddlers—a prize for the best Halloween costume, grades in school, gold stars, and on up through the university. On the job, people, teams, divisions are ranked—reward for the one at the top, punishment at the bottom. MBO, quotas, incentive pay, business plans, put together separately, division by division, cause further loss, unknown and unknowable."

Ironically, by focusing on performing for someone else's approval, corporations create the very conditions that predestine them to mediocre performance. Over the long run, superior performance depends on superior learning. A Shell study showed that, according to former planning director Arie de Geus, "a full one-third of the Fortune 500 industrials listed in 1970 had vanished by 1983." Today, the average lifetime of the largest industrial enterprises is probably less than *half* the average lifetime of a person in an industrial society. On the other hand, de Geus and his colleagues at Shell also found a small number of companies that survived for seventy-five years or longer. Interestingly, the key to their survival was the ability to run "experiments in the margin," to continually explore new business and organizational opportunities that create potential new sources of growth.

If anything, the need for understanding how organizations learn and accelerating that learning is greater today than ever before. The old days when a Henry Ford, Alfred Sloan, or Tom Watson *learned for the organization* are gone. In an increasingly dynamic, interdependent, and unpredictable world, it is simply no longer possible for anyone to "figure it all out at the top." The old model, "the top thinks and the local acts," must now give way to integrating thinking and acting at all levels. While the challenge is great, so is the potential payoff. "The person who figures out how to harness the collective genius of the people in his or her organization," according to former Citibank CEO Walter Wriston, "is going to blow the competition away."

Adaptive Learning and Generative Learning

The prevailing view of learning organizations emphasizes increased adaptability. Given the accelerating pace of change, or so the standard view goes, "the most successful corporation of the 1990s," according to *Fortune* magazine, "will be something called a learning organization, a consummately adaptive enterprise." As the Shell study shows, examples of traditional authoritarian bureaucracies that responded too slowly to survive in changing business environments are legion.

The impulse to learn, at its heart, is an impulse to be generative, to expand our capability. This is why leading corporations are focusing on *generative* learning, which is about creating, as well as *adaptive* learning, which is about coping.

The Leader's New Work

"I talk with people all over the country about learning organizations, and the response is always very positive," says William O'Brien, CEO of the Hanover Insurance companies. "If this type of organization is so widely preferred, why don't people create such organizations? I think the answer is leadership. People have no real comprehension of the type of commitment it requires to build such an organization."

Our traditional view of leaders—as special people who set the direction, make the key decisions, and energize the troops—is deeply rooted in an individualistic and nonsystemic worldview. Especially in the West, leaders are *heroes*—great men (and occasionally women) who rise to the fore in times of crisis. So long as such myths prevail, they reinforce a focus on short-term events and charismatic heroes rather than on systemic forces and collective learning.

Leadership in learning organizations centers on subtler and ultimately more important work. In a learning organization, leaders' roles differ dramatically from that of the charismatic decision maker. Leaders are designers, teachers, and stewards. These roles require new skills: the ability to build shared vision, to bring to the surface and challenge prevailing mental models, and to foster more systemic patterns of thinking. In short, leaders in learning organizations are responsible for *building organizations* where people are continually expanding their capabilities to shape their future—that is, leaders are responsible for learning.

91

Creative Tension: The Integrating Principle

Leadership in a learning organization starts with the principle of creative tension. Creative tension comes from seeing clearly where we want to be, our "vision," and telling the truth about where we are, our "current reality." The gap between the two generates a natural tension as illustrated below.

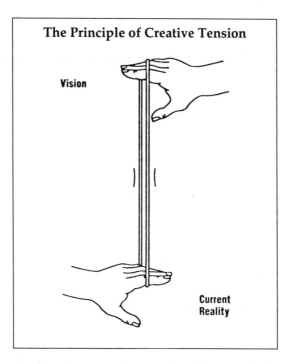

The Principle of Creative Tension

Vision

Current Reality

Creative tension can be resolved in two basic ways: by raising current reality toward the vision, or by lowering the vision toward current reality. Individuals, groups, and organizations who learn how to work with creative tension learn how to use the energy it generates to move reality more reliably toward their visions.

Without vision there is no creative tension. Creative tension cannot be generated from current reality alone. All the analysis in the world will never generate a vision. Many who are otherwise qualified to lead fail to do so because they try to substitute analysis for vision. They believe that, if only people understood current reality, they would surely feel the motivation to change. They are then disappointed to discover that people "resist" the personal and organizational changes that must be made to alter reality. What they never grasp is that the natural energy for changing reality comes from holding a picture of what might be that is more important to people than what is.

But creative tension cannot be generated from vision alone; it demands an accurate picture of current reality as well. Vision without an understanding of current reality will more likely foster cynicism than creativity. The principle of creative tension teaches that *an accurate picture of current reality is just as important as a compelling picture of a desired future.*

New Roles

The traditional authoritarian image of the leader as "the boss calling the shots" has been recognized as oversimplified and inadequate for some time. According to Edgar Schein, "Leadership is intertwined with culture formation." Building an organization's culture and shaping its evolution is the "unique and essential function" of leadership. In a learning organization, the critical roles of leadership—designer, teacher, and steward—have antecedents in the ways leaders have contributed to building organizations in the past.

Leader as Designer

What, specifically, is involved in organizational design? "Organization design is widely misconstrued as moving around boxes and lines," says Hanover's O'Brien. "The *first* task of organization design concerns designing the governing ideas of purpose, vision and core values by which people will live." Few acts of leadership have a more enduring impact on an organization than building a foundation of purpose and core values.

The *second* design task involves the policies, strategies, and structures that translate guiding ideas into business decisions. Leadership theorist Philip Selznick calls policy and structure the "institutional embodiment of purpose." "Policy making (the rules that guide decisions) ought to be separated from decision

93

making," says Jay Forrester. "Otherwise, short-term pressures will usurp time from policy creation."

Leader as Teacher

Leader as teacher does *not* mean leader as authoritarian expert whose job it is to teach people the "correct" view of reality. Rather, it is about helping everyone in the organization, oneself included, to gain more insightful views of current reality. This is in line with a popular emerging view of leaders as coaches, guides, or facilitators. In learning organizations, this teaching role is developed further by virtue of explicit attention to people's mental models and by the influence of the systems perspective.

Leader as Steward

While stewardship has long been recognized as an aspect of leadership, its source is still not widely understood. I believe Robert Greenleaf came closest to explaining real stewardship in his seminal book *Servant Leadership*. There, Greenleaf argues that "the servant leader *is* servant first. . . . It begins with the natural feeling that one wants to serve, to serve *first*. This conscious choice brings one to aspire to lead. That person is sharply different from one who is leader first, perhaps because of the need to assuage an unusual power drive or to acquire material possessions."

Leaders engaged in building learning organizations naturally feel part of a larger purpose that goes beyond their organizations. They are part of changing the way businesses operate, not from a vague philanthropic urge, but from a conviction that their efforts will produce more productive organizations, capable of achieving higher levels of organizational success and personal satisfaction than more traditional organizations. Their sense of stewardship was succinctly captured by George Bernard Shaw when he said,

> *This is the true joy in life, the being used for a purpose you consider a mighty one, the being a force of nature rather than a feverish, selfish clod of ailments and grievances complaining that the world will not devote itself to making you happy.*

New Skills

New leadership roles require new leadership skills. These skills can only be developed, in my judgment, through a lifelong commitment. It is not enough for one or two individuals to develop these skills. They must be distributed widely throughout the organization. This is one reason that understanding the *disciplines* of a learning organization is so important. These disciplines embody the principles and practices that can widely foster leadership development.

Three critical areas of skills (disciplines) are: building shared vision, surfacing and challenging mental models, and engaging in systems thinking.

Building Shared Vision

The skills involved in building shared vision include the following:

• **Encouraging Personal Vision.** Shared visions emerge from personal visions. It is not that people only care about their own self-interest—in fact, people's values usually include dimensions that concern family, organization, community, and even the world. Rather, it is that people's capacity for caring is *personal*.

• **Communicating and Asking for Support.** Leaders must be willing to continually share their own vision, rather than being the official representative of the corporate vision. They also must be prepared to ask, "Is this vision worthy of your commitment?" This can be difficult for a person used to setting goals and presuming compliance.

• **Visioning As an Ongoing Process.** Building shared vision is a never-ending process. At any one point there will be a particular image of the future that is predominant, but that image will evolve. Today, too many managers want to dispense with the "vision business" by going off and writing the Official Vision Statement. Such statements almost always lack the vitality, freshness, and excitement of a genuine vision that comes from people asking, "What do we really want to achieve?"

• **Blending Extrinsic and Intrinsic Visions.** Many energizing visions are extrinsic—that is, they focus on achieving something relative to an outsider, such as a competitor. But a goal that is limited to defeating an opponent can, once the vision is achieved, easily become a defensive posture. In contrast, intrinsic goals like creating a new type of product, taking an established product to a new level, or setting a new standard for customer satisfaction can call forth a new level of creativity and innovation. Intrinsic and extrinsic visions need to coexist; a vision solely predicated on defeating an adversary will eventually weaken an organization.

• **Distinguishing Positive from Negative Visions.** Many organizations only truly pull together when their survival is threatened. Similarly, most social movements aim at eliminating what people don't want: for example, anti-drug, anti-smoking, or anti-nuclear arms movements. Negative visions carry a subtle message of powerlessness: people will only pull together when there is sufficient threat. Negative visions also tend to be short term. Two fundamental sources of energy can motivate organizations: fear and aspiration. Fear, the energy source behind negative visions, can produce extraordinary changes in short periods, but aspiration endures as a continuing source of learning and growth.

Surfacing and Testing Mental Models

Many of the best ideas in organizations never get put into practice. One reason is that new insights and initiatives often conflict with established mental models. The leadership task of challenging assumptions without invoking defensiveness requires reflection and inquiry skills possessed by few leaders in traditional controlling organizations.

• **Seeing Leaps of Abstraction.** Our minds literally move at lightning speed. Ironically, this often slows our learning, because we leap to generalizations so quickly that we never think to test them. We then confuse our generalizations with the observable data upon which they are based, treating the generalizations *as if they were data.*

• **Balancing Inquiry and Advocacy.** Most managers are skilled at articulating their views and presenting them persuasively. While important, advocacy skills can become counterproductive as managers rise in responsibility and confront increasingly complex issues that require collaborative learning among different, equally knowledgeable people. Leaders in learning organizations need to have both inquiry *and* advocacy skills.

• **Distinguishing Espoused Theory from Theory in Use.** We all like to think that we hold certain views, but often our actions reveal deeper views. For example, I may proclaim that people are trustworthy, but never lend friends money and jealously guard my possessions. Obviously, my deeper mental model (my theory in use) differs from my espoused theory. Recognizing gaps between espoused views and theories in use (which often requires the help of others) can be pivotal to deeper learning.

• **Recognizing and Defusing Defensive Routines.** As one CEO in our research program puts it, "Nobody ever talks about an issue at the 8:00 a.m. business meeting exactly the same way they talk about it at home that evening or over drinks at the end of the day." The reason is what Chris Argyris calls "defensive routines," entrenched habits used to protect ourselves from the embarrassment and threat that come with exposing our thinking. For most of us, such defenses began to build early in life in response to pressures to have the right answers in school or at home. Organizations add new levels of performance anxiety and thereby amplify and exacerbate this defensiveness. Ironically, this makes it even more difficult to expose hidden mental models, and thereby lessens learning.

Systems Thinking

We all know that leaders should help people see the big picture. But the actual skills whereby leaders are supposed to achieve this are not well understood. In my experience, successful leaders often are "systems thinkers" to a considerable extent. They focus less on day-to-day events and more on underlying trends and forces of change. But they do this almost completely intuitively. The consequence is that they are often unable to explain their intuitions to others and feel frustrated that others cannot see the world the way they do.

One of the most significant developments in management science today is the gradual coalescence of managerial systems thinking as a field of study and practice. This field suggests some key skills for future leaders:

• **Seeing Interrelationships, Not Things, and Processes, Not Snapshots.** Most of us have been conditioned throughout our lives to focus on things and to see the world in static images. This leads us to linear explanations of systemic phenomenon.

• **Moving Beyond Blame.** We tend to blame each other or outside circumstances for our problems. But it is poorly designed systems, not incompetent or unmotivated individuals, that cause most organizational problems. Systems thinking shows us that there is no outside—that you and the cause of your problems are part of a single system

• **Distinguishing Detail Complexity from Dynamic Complexity.** Some types of complexity are more important strategically than others. Detail complexity arises when there are many variables. Dynamic complexity arises when cause and effect are distant in time and space, and when the consequences over time of interventions are subtle and not obvious to many participants in the system. The leverage in most management situations lies in understanding dynamic complexity, not detail complexity.

• **Focusing on Areas of High Leverage.** Some have called systems thinking the "new dismal science" because it teaches that most obvious solutions don't work—at best, they improve matters in the short run, only to make things worse in the long run. But there is another side to the story. Systems thinking also shows that small, well-focused actions can produce significant, enduring improvements, if they are in the right place. Systems thinkers refer to this idea as the principle of "leverage." Tackling a difficult problem is often a matter of seeing where the high leverage lies, where a change—with a minimum of effort—would lead to lasting, significant improvement.

• **Avoiding Symptomatic Solutions.** The pressures to intervene in management systems that are going awry can be overwhelming. Unfortunately, given the linear thinking that predominates in most organizations, interventions usually focus on symptomatic fixes, not underlying causes. This results in only temporary relief, and it tends to create still more pressures later on for further, low-leverage intervention. If leaders acquiesce to these pressures, they can be sucked into an endless spiral of increasing intervention. Sometimes the most difficult leadership acts are to refrain from intervening through popular quick fixes and to keep the pressure on everyone to identify more enduring solutions.

While leaders who can articulate systemic explanations are rare, those who *can* will leave their stamp on an organization.

The consequences of leaders who lack systems thinking skills can be devastating. Many charismatic leaders manage almost exclusively at the level of events. They deal in visions and in crises, and little in between. Under their leadership, an organization hurtles from crisis to crisis. Eventually, the worldview of people in the organization becomes dominated by events and reactiveness. Many, especially those who are deeply committed, become burned out. Eventually, cynicism comes to pervade the organization. People have no control over their time, let alone their destiny.

Similar problems arise with the "visionary strategist," the leader with vision who sees both patterns of change and events. This leader is better prepared to manage change. He or she can explain strategies in terms of emerging trends and thereby foster a climate that is less reactive. But such leaders still impart a responsive orientation rather than a generative one.

Many talented leaders have rich, highly systemic intuitions but cannot explain those intuitions to others. Ironically, they often end up being authoritarian leaders, even if they don't want to, because only they see the decisions that need to be made. They are unable to conceptualize their strategic insights so that these can become public knowledge, open to challenge and further improvement.

New Tools

Developing the skills described above requires new tools—tools that will enhance leaders' conceptual abilities and foster communication and collaborative inquiry.

Systems Archetypes

One of the insights of the budding, managerial systems-thinking field is that certain types of systemic structures recur again and again. Countless systems grow for a period, then encounter problems and cease to grow (or even collapse) well before they have reached intrinsic limits to growth. Many other systems get locked in runaway vicious spirals where every actor has to run faster and faster to stay in the same place. Still others lure individual actors into doing what seems right locally, yet which eventually causes suffering for all.

Charting Strategic Dilemmas

Management teams typically come unglued when confronted with core dilemmas. A classic example was the way U.S. manufacturers faced the low cost-high quality choice. For years, most assumed that it was necessary to choose between the two. Not surprisingly, given the short-term pressures perceived by most managements, the prevailing choice was low cost. Firms that chose high quality usually perceived themselves as aiming exclusively for a high-quality, high-price market niche. The consequences of this perceived either-or choice have been disastrous, even fatal, as U.S. manufacturers have encountered increasing international competition from firms that have chosen to consistently improve quality *and* cost.

Developing Leaders and Learning Organizations

In a recently published retrospective on organization development in the 1980s, Marshall Sashkin and N. Warner Burke observe the return of an emphasis on developing leaders who can develop organizations. They also note Schein's critique that most top executives are not qualified for the task of developing culture. Learning organizations represent a potentially significant evolution of organizational culture. So it should come as no surprise that such organizations will remain a distant vision until the leadership capabilities they demand are developed. "The 1990s may be the period," suggest Sashkin and Burke, "during which organization development and (a new sort of) management development are reconnected."

I believe that this new sort of management development will focus on the roles, skills, and tools for leadership in learning organizations. Undoubtedly, the ideas offered above are only a rough approximation of this new territory. The sooner we begin seriously exploring the territory, the sooner the initial map can be improved—and the sooner we will realize an age-old vision of leadership:

The wicked leader is he who the people despise.
The good leader is he who the people revere.
The great leader is he who the people say, "We did it ourselves."

— Lao Tsu

TERRY MOLLNER, Ed.D., is founder and chair of Massachusetts-based Trusteeship Institute, Inc., which consults with corporations converting to the Relationship Age worldview. Trusteeship Institute assists firms at any stage in the process of converting to employee-ownership using an employee stock ownership plan (ESOP).

Dr. Mollner is a founding board member of the Calvert Social Investment Fund and a fellow of the World Business Academy. He is currently writing a book for Doubleday with the working title of *All is Relationship, Not Matter: The Emergence of the Corporate Tribe.*

7

The 21st-Century Corporation:
The Tribe of the Relationship Age

Terry Mollner

The story of the '60s generation is usually told mainly as one of liberation: sexual liberation, another surge in the liberation of women from a second-class status, the liberation from dogmas and the broadening of forms of spiritual expression, wide experimentation in life-styles, living arrangements, music, art, and love. All this did, indeed, occur. However, now, with the gift of hindsight and the perspective of greater maturity, we can see that the main story is not one of liberation. Rather it is a sad story. It is the story of a generation that realized that there no longer were any elders.

Elders are people who consistently give priority to the common good in all their affairs, who join in communities where this is clearly the highest priority, who inspire the young to want to become members of their communities, and who successfully initiate them into a life within the community of elders that feels full of meaning. They also view the world as tribes within tribes, take greater direct responsibility for the welfare of those concentric circles of tribes closest to them, and always behave in ways consistent with the common good of all of nature and humanity.

With no one leading us into a meaningful life, we had no choice but to leave home, family, and community in order to find home, family, and community. Psychologically, not geographically, most of us prodigal children returned. Some of us found the answer to the question "What is a meaningful life?" on our own. However, many of us did not, at least not yet.

The phenomenon of separation (of everyone from everyone else) in our culture did not begin with the '60s generation. According to many, it began with the Industrial Revolution and perhaps well before that. The emergence of a third category between child and adult called "adolescence" was perhaps the first way we tried to become conscious of it. But the '60s generation was also the first television generation. Thus, we were able to be aware of each other's activities beyond the local area as no other generation had been able to be. Through television our village had suddenly expanded from our town to the globe without the creation of a global village system of governance and eldering. Our local elders dropped from the giant stars of our childhood to bit players on a movie production set so large that they hadn't yet met any of those who had lines to speak. The global village did not appear to be connected to our local community, and rather than giving it any legitimacy, it did the opposite. It sucked all the vital energy out of it. Legitimacy was on Wall Street, in Hollywood, on Madison Avenue, in Washington, D.C., in the executive offices of the multinational corporations or in the labs of the great universities.

The Two Possible Fundamental Worldviews

Throughout history there have been two fundamental worldviews that have competed for a consensus. I believe that all other worldviews, theories, philosophies, theologies, social and economic theories, etc. can be traced back to one of these two possible fundamental worldviews. I call them the Material Age worldview and the Relationship Age worldview and define them as follows:

MATERIAL AGE worldview: (two-or-moreness) the assumption that the universe is somewhere between two and an immense number of *separate parts* each of which *competes* for its own self-interest in relation to all other things. (Evolution is the result of the survival of the fittest through competition.)

RELATIONSHIP AGE worldview: (oneness) the assumption that the universe is an immense number of *connected parts*, each of which *cooperates* with all other parts in the interest of the universe first and only secondly cooperates or competes in the interest of itself or any sub-group of parts. (Evolution is the result of the cooperation of all things for the maturation of the one whole.)

The Cooperative Maturation Continuum below represents the range of human behaviors in terms of these two possible fundamental worldviews:

The Cooperative Maturation Continuum

			SELF- CONSCIOUS	SELF- CONSCIOUS
WAR <—COMPETITION—ENLIGHTENED—CONSCIOUS—>CONSCIOUS				
		SELF-INTEREST	COOPERATION	HARMONY
competition unto death - lowest skill of self- consciously or unconsciously cooperating as one with all things	belief in separate parts with differing degrees of restraints	compromise- belief in separate parts as real but attempting cooperation	belief in no separate parts, with differing degrees of competition allowed	cooperation which is total, self-conscious, and effortless- highest skill of self- consciously cooperating as one with all things

MATERIAL AGE
<————Competitive Continuum————>
(assume two-or-moreness to be real)
("self" is defined as less than the universe)

RELATIONSHIP AGE
<————————Cooperative Continuum————————>
(assume oneness to be real)
("self" is defined as the universe)

Lowest		Highest
Level of<——————————————————————————>Level of		
Human		Human
Maturity		Maturity

105

If the Relationship Age worldview is correct and all things are, indeed, parts of a whole, then war and competition are not alternatives to cooperation; rather, they are the lower forms of cooperation. If the universe is one thing, it is not possible to escape the interrelatedness of nature with all its interdependent parts moving and relating as parts of the whole. Survival of the fittest through competition is the highest level of cooperative relationship possible by non-self-conscious parts.

Competition is an illusion created by humans. It does not exist in nature. Nature is at all times solely cooperative. The perception of competition is but the projection of the Material Age worldview onto what we are witnessing. As separate parts, they are, indeed, competing. As parts of one whole, they are cooperating. Which you see is determined by your self-definition. From the perspective of the Relationship Age self-definition, competition is the word we give to the lowest form of cooperation. It is not an alternative to it. Cooperation is fundamental in nature. It has no alternative.

Moving from left to right on the Cooperative Maturation Continuum is moving from less mature forms of cooperation to more mature forms, from war at one extreme to self-conscious harmony at the other extreme. By choosing the Material Age worldview, we have locked ourselves into the experiences at the lowest level of maturity. Compromise, where neither side in a relationship feels fully satisfied, is the most mature experience available to us. This is the behavior we would call "loving," whether at home, at work, or anywhere else.

However, once the Relationship Age worldview is chosen, the experiences on the second half of the continuum become viewed as possibilities rather than as naive fantasies, unattainable but worthy of pursuit. Our view of what is possible in an organization, partnership, friendship, or loving relationship changes, and, of course, we now demand more than a willingness to compromise in our most intimate or important relationships. We now want the self-conscious feeling of togetherness as parts of one thing that has no opposite. This is the feeling of true love, which we are forever seeking because we have had it for fleeting moments while operating in the Material Age self-definition. We remember those particular moments with one other human being where the feeling of oneness was present because our focus of attention was solely on that particular relationship and, for those moments, in the pattern of oneness. In part, this probably explains the large increase in divorce in our society and is additional evidence that we are moving into the Relationship Age. It also explains the demand for more mature relationships in the workplace and the decline of the competitive ethic encouraged up until recently by both management and unions. People have come to believe that it is possible to agree, disagree, sort things out, and make decisions as a secondary activity within a continuous loving context rather than at the expense of it.

As mentioned earlier, in the Material Age worldview each person has a different top priority from everyone else: the top priority of each person at all times is his or her own self-interest. Whereas with the Relationship Age worldview all people and things have the same top priority at all times—the good of the one whole. It is this that allows for continuous peace rather than conflict within relationships. And it is this that allows all to feel their self-interests are fully and continuously satisfied, rather than partially and periodically satisfied. And this is the one and only top priority that will allow an individual or group to have this experience.

If the top priority is only the good of our couple, group, or corporation, we will eventually have to enter into a relationship that is primarily competitive rather than secondarily competitive with others or another group. The result is a living contradiction—we play by one set of rules at one place and time and by the opposite set of rules on another occasion. Consistency and credibility go out the window and people in our group will revert to giving priority to the self-interest of their body within our group as well. We would be a Relationship Age group in name only. Either the top priority is the good of all or it is not. And because of the nature of the mind, which projects its beliefs and sees what it believes rather than what is, if we do not succeed in changing our self-definition to the Relationship Age self-definition, we will not experience it as natural and healthy to give priority to the general welfare. Rather it will feel as it has felt in our personal Material Age past when we have tried to act for the common good: something we are forcing ourselves to do because we think we should. You cannot be a Relationship Age group sometimes. You either have one self-definition or the other.

The rite of passage ritual, at least as a meaningful experience for this purpose, has been all but totally lost in our modern Material Age societies. This is mainly because the adult community does not understand the importance of choosing between the two possible fundamental self-identities and the embracing of the Relationship Age one as part of the maturation process. In fact, quite to the contrary, we have taken pride in championing the Material Age worldview. I believe this is the main reason for the high levels of loneliness, alienation, violence, lawlessness, and self-destructive behavior that exist in our societies. But, as a result of the recent discoveries of science, I believe that this is all about to change.

What is eldering?

It should be clear by now that eldering is the process of initiating the young into this mature understanding of who they are. However, to do this one must have credibility.

Children, still so close to their unconscious and instinctual behaviors, know that giving priority to one's individual self-interest is not the answer to the question "What makes a life meaningful?" They may eventually follow someone who is a champion of the Material Age approach to life but only until they can become king of the mountain of which the leader is currently king. In terms of a meaningful life, this will have taken them around in a circle and left them right back where they started. Unless there are credible elders who can bring the Relationship Age self-identity to them in a way in which they can appreciate it and eventually embrace it, they will naturally strike out on their own before, during, or after going in this circle to find the answer to the question: to find out how to turn the line that became a circle into a spiral with no beginning or end. This will often be seen as rebellious behavior by the communities, or pseudo-communities, unable to elder them or as a mid-life crisis in older people.

So the next question becomes the following.

Who are the elders of today?

The state? Not likely. Our current nation states are primarily defined by geography. The possibility that all the people living on a certain hunk of dirt will come to agree on the Relationship Age worldview is remote. As a result of being defined by geography, our modern industrial democratic societies are locked into decision by compromise between competing forces for a long time to come. All who are members of the Relationship Age group must share its self-definition as a result of free choice. Thus it must be easy for them to leave the group if they do not or join it if they do. This is not the case with those who are in a group as a result of living in the same geographical area.

The church? Not likely but not because they wouldn't like to be. When church and state were separated, we became a schizophrenic society. One of our "selves" operated on the Material Age worldview and another on the Relationship Age worldview. The separation of church and state, a relatively new idea in human history, was mainly a choice for the Material Age worldview as the basis for society. This was more a result of the discrediting of the Relationship Age worldview by religious organizations, which continually created subjectively determined dogmas, than it was an embracing of the Material Age worldview. Science emerged as a response. Science—the search for truth for truth's sake—is the actual but unofficial spokesperson for God in our modern cultures, and its conclusions will be the basis for the building of the new Relationship Age culture. But science is an art, not an organization. So it will play an important role but is unable to serve as the Relationship Age community that will elder its children. And lacking secular authority, the religions are locked into a cheerleader role unless they once again move into secular activities. This is not likely to be the dominant approach in the West, although we have been witnessing it occurring in Muslim nations. Iran is the obvious example.

Our blood families? Perhaps, but with difficulty, mainly because now that we are so far removed from an agricultural society, the members of our families easily scatter to different geographic locations, which greatly reduces the bonding. Also, the bonding is a material bonding— blood—rather than agreement on the Relationship Age worldview. Fathers and mothers will, by default, attempt to do it for their own children, but the nuclear family unit is not a large enough unit to be easily successful. There is a need for elders and mentors other than the parents who have many entanglements with their children that qualify their ability to play this role alone. New "tribes by agreement" may emerge as a result of people in a locality bonding with their friends to create Relationship Age Tribes. I have been a member of one such tribe for nearly nine years now and we have begun to focus on the task of eldering our young. However, we do not have the additional bond of working together to provide for our material needs.

Who else could do it? It would have to be a group of people who create a group based upon agreement rather than geography, nationality, race, or any other material reason. Secondly, it will have to be a group that people can join or leave easily. Thirdly, it will have to be a group that is comfortable having its actions spring from a worldview it chooses. And, finally, it will have to be a group that is materially self-sufficient in financial terms—not subsistence living terms—so it will be independent. In modern society the group that best fulfills these criteria is the private corporation.

As private corporations assume the Relationship Age worldview, they will become tribes that transcend the boundaries of geographic nations and will be encouraged by those nations because they will solve many of the chronic social problems unsolvable by geographic definition alone. "For-profit" will be replaced with "for-good" as the top priority, not out of idealism but out of a recognition that they have been giving it priority all along and are unable to do otherwise. Placing "for the common good" as their top priority will still leave "for-profit" as a secondary priority but it will be an acknowledgment that the company now chooses to operate at the more mature end of the Cooperative Maturation Continuum rather than at the lower end. The result should be higher profits than when "for-profit" was the top priority as a result of being able to route the most mature spirit of its members into their work. Employees will live for work as well as for the weekends. Work will cease to be a means of survival and become a means of joining with others in extending creation because it will now be experienced as connected to all of creation in a meaningful way.

As all wise business people have known for thousands of years, the marketplace is not primarily a center of competitive activity but of cooperative activity. The ruse that companies are primarily competing will be dropped. The marketplace, like everything else in nature, is fundamentally cooperative.

The Japanese and Germans are way ahead of us in recognizing and acting on this truth, although usually still for their self-interests. Especially in Japan, mainly as a result of a different cultural heritage, self-interest is not primarily their private interest; it is their national interest. Japan operates as a conglomerate Material Age tribe, whereas American corporations still operate as independent companies.

Our modern nation states are societies based on agreements, usually called "laws." All relationships occur within these agreements, or one is not allowed to play by being put in jail. In the marketplace, the free and orderly exchange of goods and services at a negotiated price necessitates the absence of a free-for-all. The conscious or unconscious agreement not to have a free-for-all is the cooperative agreement within which the free market exists. Unless you are at war with someone unto death, you are operating within some degree of restraints that are cooperative agreements. Free markets, therefore, necessitate a social contract that allows agreements to be made, facilities and distribution networks built and maintained, products

111

produced, investments made and profits distributed, etc., all on a continuous basis. Competition may be where the focus is, but cooperation is fundamental and primary.

In a Material Age society the dominant organizations cooperate for their self-interest relative to the rest. Chrysler and certain large banks were just a few of many companies too big for the government to allow them to go bankrupt, while many smaller companies and banks have to live by the rules of the supposedly primarily competitive marketplace. The fundamental policy in market sectors is also cooperation. The top priority, most visible to the general public in the airline industry, is to cooperate with their competitors for their joint interest and only secondly compete with one another for their self-interest. For instance, major airlines will all lower their fares on certain routes to force a new upstart airline out of business. OPEC is by far the most glaring example of cooperation between supposed competitors for their collective self-interest. Without this cooperation a barrel of oil would sell for $10 rather than usually double that figure.

Seven Steps

I have identified seven steps toward becoming a Relationship Age corporation:

1. honesty and openness,

2. fairness within the existing market context,

3. corporate participation in fulfilling non-work-related needs of employees and the community,

4. employee participation in profits and losses,

5. employee participation in management based on the Relationship Age worldview,

6. employee participation in the spirit of ownership within the Relationship Age worldview, and

7. democratic employee ownership and control within the Relationship Age worldview.

There are many companies that are far down this path, even though most still use the rhetoric of the Material Age: everything is justified in terms of the bottom line (increasing profits) rather than the top line (the common good). Few have reached the fifth level mainly because few have openly embraced the Relationship Age worldview. Some have tried many organizational development techniques to increase productivity. Some have been successful and some not, but all have necessitated a significant commitment of time and energy to succeed mainly because they are not able to call on the depth of commitment and wisdom that can only come from converting to the Relationship Age self-identity.

By the way, the absence the Relationship Age self-definition is also why most efforts to convert to democratic ownership and control have not fulfilled their promise. Five, fifty, five hundred, or five hundred thousand people who each have a different top priority will always be at odds with one another and only secondly cooperate for their enlightened self-interest no matter what the words or legal structure used. Obviously, therefore, a company that has one person in control with everyone else following orders will be more successful. The employees will each have a different priority, but through wages and incentives it will be tied in varying degrees to the success of the company. Also, this policy of enlightened self-interest and power hierarchy is viewed by all who hold the Material Age self-definition as natural and healthy. If management, employees, and union officials all share this worldview, the odds are good that this system will out-perform a democratically controlled company where all involved are also operating on the Material Age worldview.

Democracy will only make sense when people have succeeded in switching to the Relationship Age self-definition. Then they will not be satisfied with the partial fulfillment available to them within the Material Age organization. They will desire and seek the experiences on the second half of the Cooperative Maturation Continuum—the joy of mutually placing the common good as their highest priority; the security of self-determination in the work place through democratic means; the continuous primary feelings of connection, peace, and meaningfulness instead of alienation, stress, and meaninglessnes, etc. Mainly it will be experienced as fully rather than partially satisfying the self-interests of the individuals. This will be the result of defining their self-interests differently so they all have the same top priority—the common good. Comfortably being part of such a never-ending process is fully satisfying rather than partially satisfying.

Although it is inevitable that many of our biggest corporations will someday be democratically owned and controlled, we are still very far away from that. The next step will be the movement into stage five and six, where companies will remain owned by a few but committed to the Relationship Age self-definition.

In other words, companies will become tribes that attend to all the needs of tribe members and do so in a way that is beneficial to those inside and outside the tribe. Corporations will spawn divisions totally unrelated to the product with which the company was originally identified, such as a blues band or handicrafts, because they will be activities desired by people in the tribe. The corporation will become more of a management and commercial and social entrepreneurial center than a product center. The corporation will join with other for-profit and nonprofit corporations, usually ones it creates, into an association to meet all the needs of people in the company and in the community. And because of the Relationship Age worldview, the importance of initiating the young into it will be given great importance so they will not remain in the Material Age any longer than necessary.

Will our current generations be the ones that bring about this transformation in our society? Will those of us who feel certain that we have found the answer to the big question create a culture that initiates our young into the more mature half of life in the ways we were not? I don't know, but thirty or forty years from now we will all know the answers to these questions. Personally I think we are equal to the task, and I think it would be very much unlike us not to take it on.

114

Dr. Robert H. Rosen is a clinical psychologist, president of Healthy Companies in Washington, D.C., and assistant clinical professor of Psychiatry and Behavioral Sciences at the George Washington University School of Medicine. In early 1991, he received a multiyear grant from the MacArthur Foundation to research, disseminate, and implement new models of healthy work for the year 2000.

He has been a consultant to dozens of Fortune 500 companies, government agencies, labor unions, and hospitals and gives frequent speeches before corporations and associations.

In recent years he has appeared in the *New York Times, Washington Post, USA Today, The Wall Street Journal, Chicago Tribune, Working Woman,* plus numerous local and national television and radio appearances. Dr. Rosen is the author of over twenty articles in his field and has completed a new book entitled *The Healthy Company,* to be published in late 1991 by Tarcher/St. Martin's Press.

8

The Anatomy of a Healthy Company

Robert H. Rosen

Imagine going to work, walking into your office or plant, and encountering a vibrant, stimulating atmosphere. In talking to employees about an upcoming deadline or project, you hear only enthusiasm and commitment. They are eager to work hard, listen to your vision and strategy, and graciously share ideas. Some of the employees brainstorm about possible glitches and how to boost sales and profits. They banter with you and among themselves, their easy humor showing that they enjoy their work and that they like and respect you.

As the day progresses, they are on the phone, meeting among themselves, intent at the computer, sometimes coming to you with creative ideas or special requests. Each assignment is approached with a sense of urgency. These diligent employees are continuously looking for ways to improve their product or service, to deliver it faster and better, and to upgrade their skills.

When someone volunteers to take charge, others are quick to join in to help. They know that on another project, they may be the leader and need support. They're confident that you value their input: you listen to their suggestions and are flexible enough to accommodate each of them. The atmosphere is charged by employee voices that are sincere and remarkably human and personal. No awkward silences when bosses pass by. No secretive scribbling of cover-your-ass memos. No sullen hostility between employees competing for bigger budgets and more attention. The usual Me-versus-You antagonism has been replaced by a sharing of responsibilities and a feeling of "We're all in this together." Teamwork and partnerships, rather than the old rigid ladders, make up the company structure.

Perhaps most remarkable about this new atmosphere is a feeling of respect. From the flexible schedules to the fair salaries and benefits to the sharing of vital information, the company shows that it truly cares about people, and employees reciprocate this trust with loyalty.

This sketch is what I call a healthy company. This kind of organization may sound farfetched—a corporate utopia that only dreamers or the very naive would believe in. For many companies, it is. But among the millions of businesses in this country, some are quietly, decisively transforming themselves into healthy companies. They're driven by an unshakable conviction that only a healthy company will be alive and competitive in the coming years.

Potent Pressures

Why is it imperative that we grow healthy companies? As I travel around the country visiting organizations, I see them struggling with five potent forces that are redefining the nature of American business. A handful of companies have already recognized and capitalized on these. Others feel the pressures but do not know how to channel them into future plans. Still others do not even see them, and if and when they do, it may be too late. Companies that ignore these or underestimate their impact do so at their peril. These five forces are: (1) the Power of People, (2) the Changing Complexion of the Workplace, (3) the Dynamic Blender, (4) the New Psychological Contract, and (5) the Human crisis.

The Power of People

The power of people is perhaps the most potent force, for it reaches into all facets of all kinds of businesses, touching every stage of operations and every strategy, goal, or vision. All companies are affected, regardless of how many employees they have—from the five-person ad agency to the ten-thousand-plus manufacturing firm. In its simplest form, the power of people is replacing traditional assumptions that other tangibles, such as financing, markets, or technology, determine the course of a company. The new reality is that how people work, think, and feel dictate the direction and success of a business.

Because individuals are contributing more and more to the lifeblood of companies, the costs of mismanaging them can only drain companies. Management can choose either to treat people as valuable assets to be maintained and improved upon or to continue the hemorrhaging and treat people as costly liabilities that increasingly demand more money for health claims, accidents, mediocrity, and replacement.

A Company of Strangers

The changing complexion of the workplace is the second force. Soon the typical American worker will not be a white, middle-aged man but a collage of people—women, Blacks, Hispanics, Asians, older workers, and the disabled. Although ethnically rich, this diverse work force confronts years of singular thinking, opening up potential conflicts and misunderstandings. Old assumptions about people's training, schooling, values, and cultural backgrounds are no longer operative and must be discarded for a new openness and flexibility. In a company of strangers, both management and co-workers need to learn about each other and strive to meld everyone into a unified and multitalented work force.

The Dynamic Blender

I call the third force the Dynamic Blender. In a word, it is high-pressure, lightning-like *change*. From the suddenly omnipresent fax machine to the marketing opportunities created by the economic revolution in Eastern Europe, in some companies,

119

the accelerating and never-ending pace of change is little understood and therefore badly managed.

Most of us are struggling to understand, accommodate, and benefit from change; but in the process, we can become easily burned-out, stretched beyond limits, and over-stressed. The companies and managers who see the opportunities in this so-called blender—who learn how to work with different kinds of employees, navigate the human side of change, and take advantage of technological and competitive breakthroughs—will escape the suffering of misjudging and mismanaging the power of this force.

The New Psychological Contract

Another subtle but powerful force is a new psychological contract between employee and company that is redefining traditional understandings about promises, loyalties, working relationships, and roles. From the corporate view, this new contract recognizes that employers can no longer offer lifetime jobs, guaranteed advancement, or kindly paternalism. Economic survival demands that they be able to expand and contract quickly and be flexible enough to respond to changing markets and global opportunities.

But companies need committed employees in order to react quickly to the marketplace, and they need these fast reflexes at a time when employee cynicism, mistrust, and self-interest are ubiquitous. So employers must offer a new contract that gives the company this flexibility, but at the same time presents employees with more chances for personal and professional growth. Employees will accept the new contract only with the provisos that their employers are honest, open, and fair with them and that they have a larger say in their jobs.

The Human Crisis

This force refers to the need for a dramatic expansion of companies' roles and responsibilities to incorporate the whole employee, not simply the person who works eight hours a day. This crisis demands that companies begin to pay attention to employees' minds, bodies, relationships, and families. Companies that ignore the total person will receive a very painful lesson in the costs of employing a person who has physical and/ or mental ailments, or whose family life is a source of stress.

Some companies are trying to address this crisis through expanded benefit programs. The old narrowly defined health insurance and pension packages are now considered entitlements, so employers are developing a broader set of work-life benefits.

While this trend certainly increases a company's attractiveness to new employees, it marks just the beginning of confronting the crisis. Employees also want more compassion and opportunity at work, more enlightened attitudes and behavior—in short, a corporate mentality that recognizes and appreciates the human side of its business as much as the financial side.

When I talk to both CEOs and employees, I hear a litany of complaints, suspicion, and pain. By and large, employees feel alienated, shut out of the company "loop" and its corporate mission, and disenfranchised by employers who demand more, impose dehumanizing bureaucracies, and operate according to capricious rules and regulations. Their psychological needs for self-esteem, growth, and well-being are not being met. Employees deeply believe that their personal values are at odds with what's important and worthwhile to their employers. They hear CEOs make speeches about fairness and equality, then learn about astronomical executive pay packages. They hear about a company's invigorating spirit of competitiveness, then find that office politics, not professional excellence, reap the biggest promotions.

For managers, the pain is twofold: it comes from above— from senior executives who insist that they show results immediately, while simultaneously cutting back, and it comes from below—from employees who lack a sense of urgency and responsibility, shirk their duties, and are apathetic about their work. Managers are caught in between, grappling with the limitations of unskilled employees and dysfunctional teams, and trying to tame the tensions generated by rapid change. To

121

cope and survive, many of them feel forced into hoarding their power and looking out only for themselves. Thus, despite many managers' conviction that they are good people managers, their management style is controlling and self-centered.

The company pain is most obvious. You can see it in escalating costs of labor and benefits eating away at profits and operating budgets; in declining productivity and morale; in high turnover rates and poor recruiting results; and in a lagging ability to innovate and compete internationally. This pain is also apparent in the inability of companies to check out social problems, from AIDS to illiteracy, many of which have invaded the workplace and undermined the work force.

Each of these participants—employees, managers, companies—suffers from inertia and resistance. They dislike the status quo but balk at changing their ways. Encircling this situation is an ever-widening gap between what people say they believe and value and how they behave.

Why have we allowed ourselves, our employees, and our companies to become this way? To understand, we need to examine some antiquated attitudes about people and management. For decades, companies have operated on the belief that immediate productivity and profits were more important than people, that shareholders were more important than employees. They pushed for instant, transitory rewards and ignored the potential of seasoned development of people and products.

In this environment, employees have been regarded as costly liabilities that were constantly depleting and had to be pushed and shoved for maximum output. If the past decade had a motto, it was "profits at any price," and the price it paid was a slipshod work force, defective goods and services, and a faltering future.

But the future begins today, and if all of us, individuals and institutions, do not invest in our work force now, this shortsightedness will haunt us for decades to come. Our workplaces will become even more painful places to work, and American business will shrivel up.

What Is a Healthy Company?

By now you probably have a pretty good picture of what a healthy company is *not*—the mismanaged personal and business pressures, coupled with the consequences it has inflicted, offer a graphic illustration of the guts of an unhealthy company.

A healthy company, on the other hand, is much more than simply the absence of these forces and feelings. Just like a fine athlete is more than someone who isn't sick, a healthy company embodies people and practices that combine and coordinate to produce an exceptional performance.

Healthy companies all possess and emanate a certain vitality and spirit. This spirit is not a religious fervor or a mindless cheerleader enthusiasm but a deep feeling of shared humanistic values at the core of the company. These values are the glue that binds healthy, successful employees with healthy, productive workplaces. They influence the way people act and think at all levels of the company and form the foundation for corporate policies and practices. They define roles and responsibilities and dictate how business decisions are made. These principles are expressed and applied at every turn of the business, from receptionists and loading dock workers, through managers and executives, and into the board of directors.

These values are perpetually interacting, expanding, and contracting like a living entity. Each value depends on and determines the health of the others; sickness or disease that undermines one weakens all; robustness in one value strengthens all. The values at the heart of a healthy company enable it to continuously grow, evolve, and renew itself, reinforcing what is productive and positive and sloughing off the unhealthy and unworkable. In short, the causes and effects between values, people, and companies are not linear but circular. Values *are* the center of the enterprise; they circulate through every cell and artery of a company, and a company and its employees either reinforce healthy values or bring about their decline.

Healthy company values bind people to their organizations. By creating a common language and appealing to prin-

123

ciples of dignity, commitment, and growth, these values help to create an identity that connects thousands of people around a shared mission. Suddenly, the traditional hard values of business success and the nontraditional soft values of human development merge into one dream.

This convergence generates a synergy, producing something greater than the sum of their parts—a vital business that lives and breathes a humanistic philosophy, that treats people as more than profit producers, views relationships as more than simply financial contracts, and regards the workplace as more than a setting for business. It is a holistic environment, one that nurtures, stretches, and empowers people. The result is an organization that optimizes people, principles, and profits. Here are the key values that people hold in the healthy company:

Commitment to Self-Knowledge and Development

This value is a commitment to one's own personal growth and understanding. On a personal level, people with this value are introspective, principle driven, and constantly learning about themselves. Managers translate this learning into leadership that inspires both personal and professional development in employees.

Organizations dedicated to self-knowledge are learning institutions. Their value of people as appreciating assets, not costly liabilities, overshadows all other decisions. Through a broad, caring human capital investment strategy, executives make large investments in training; managers cultivate employee effectiveness and their successors; and employees learn to innovate and take risks. For these companies, managing learning is a full-time job, and for their companies to grow each year, every employee must grow and develop.

Firm Belief in Decency

The basic precept here is decency: people who naturally and instinctively treat others as would any feeling, thinking human being, as they would like to be treated. This value is founded on the conviction that people work best when they are respected, when they are genuinely appreciated for what they bring to a company.

In these healthy companies, actions speak louder than words, promises are kept, discrepancies between what managers say and what they do rarely surface, and half-truths, prevarications, or deceptions are not tolerated. Managers are honest with employees, sharing their knowledge and even feelings; and they are fair, apportioning rewards and criticism according to accomplishments and deeds. Openness is a ground rule for all relationships. Regardless of the forum, the feedback is always candid, helpful, fair, and constant.

Respect for Individual Differences

People who respect individual differences know that an office is populated by individuals who look different, act different, grew up in different cultures, but who are just as capable and worthwhile. Rather than insisting that everyone conform to a white, middle-class norm, employees and managers value the richness, diversity, and imaginative ideas dissimilar people bring to their jobs.

Companies show their respect by not promoting policies or tacit standards that imply a homogeneous work force. For example, glass ceilings have doors that open for women and minorities; work schedules are flexible enough to accommodate all kinds of families; and employees are encouraged to express their personal differences. There are no second-class citizens, only human beings of equal worth with special roles and responsibilities.

Spirit of Partnership

This value is a strong belief in "community," in the strength of shared effort, in the value of teamwork, in the satisfaction of partnership. Though personally capable, both manager and employee truly believe that two minds are better than one, and many minds are best. They make great team players and form strong relationships because they understand the dynamics of giving and taking, leading and following.

Together, a responsible employee and an empowering manager form a special team—an entrepreneurial partnership of adults dedicated to mobilizing each others' talents and producing results. This group is not a collection of Indians and one chief, but a collaboration of co-equals, with individuals stepping forward to take the lead when they have more experience, specialized knowledge, or unique creative talents. This partnership's motto is "Everyone is a leader, everyone is a follower."

High Priority for Health and Well-being

Healthy employees are a company's most valuable asset. Like a well-crafted piece of precision equipment, employees must be maintained and polished—from reducing the level of their cholesterol to giving them time for family matters.

Inherent in this value is the certainty that work can either make people sick or improve their health. The physical and psychological climate at work—the size of the computer screen, the interior air, the level of boredom in a job, the attitudes of supervisors—plays an enormous role in well-being and performance.

At the company level, health and well-being are emphasized through adequate health and disability coverage, wellness and employee assistance programs, flexible scheduling, family leave policies, competitive and equitable pay, and profit sharing. Safety too is a concern, and healthy companies do more than tout the importance of safety—they institute practical, vital safeguards in every corner of the workplace.

Appreciation for Flexibility and Resilience

This value is founded on the inevitability of change and the necessity of taking charge of any natural evolution, be it financial, technological, or personal. Resilient employees exhibit this value in their attitude toward new situations and obstacles. They ask plenty of questions and are not easily discouraged. Rich with capability, not conformity, they don't avoid the tough jobs or duck responsibility. When they do get overwhelmed, their spirit, vitality, and winning attitude guide them through the hard times.

Managers with this value know that regardless of what an employee actually does every day, whether it's mundane or unique, manual or mental, people need variety, flexibility, and a sense of completion and ownership. The healthy company reinforces this value through a variety of offerings: they give employees the tools so they can cope with change; they provide advance notice of layoffs and relocations; and they make the transition as smooth as possible.

Passion for Products and Process

With a clear mission and plan of action, people with a passion for products are active, effective doers. They set goals, benchmarks, and timetables and know where they're going and why. These people *care* what happens to their company— they feel personally involved and responsible for its successes and failures.

However, their passion for outcome does not interfere with their respect for process. Although persistent and competitive, they care as much about how they produce something as the product itself; as driven as they are, they know they must take into account the interests and needs of all their constituents.

That is why patience and persistence are essential—a natural outcome of their strong belief in people, their respect for relationships, and their commitment to the company's long-term mission. Experience has shown them that even if they achieve quick results, these results are often transitory and often undermine personal and economic success.

Ultimately, the healthy company views products and profits not as their immediate goal, but rather the result of doing everything else right. Their economic success—improved quality, better service, competitive advantage are the by-products of shared values and collective effort.

These values are the lifeblood of a healthy company—they flow through the arteries of the organization. Each employee, manager, and executive must decide how to put these values to work. Regardless of the size of your work group or your location on the corporate ladder, what happens to these values is in your hands.

Incorporating values entails bringing about a metamorphosis, beginning first with yourself, then applying them to your immediate work surroundings, and ultimately spreading them throughout your company. You will find that the insights and suggestions originate on the personal level, then grow larger and outward to include your role in the company, and finally encompass your entire company's beliefs and activities.

If you assimilate these values as your own, and live and work by them as practical, sensible guidelines, you will be healthy and so will your company.

JUANITA BROWN is president of Whole Systems Associates, an international consulting consortium dedicated to strategic change management. She has worked with corporate clients throughout the United States, Europe, and Latin America, including Kraft General Foods, Procter & Gamble, Scandinavian Airlines System (SAS), Exxon, Hewlett-Packard, and the National Bank of Mexico.

Ms. Brown is a fellow of the World Business Academy and has served as program faculty at the John F. Kennedy University School of Management and at the California Institute of Integral Studies. Ms. Brown's latest article, "Leading as Learning," has been published in *Transforming Leadership: From Vision to Results*, a book exploring cutting-edge developments in leadership theory and practice.

David Isaacs, president of Clearing Communications and a partner in Whole Systems Associates, as well as Sue Kreger of Whole Systems Associates, collaborated in writing this chapter.

9

Corporation As Community:
A New Image for a New Era

Juanita Brown

*There is no such thing as an inevitable form of organiza-
tion. . . . Organizations are free to seek transformations
in conventional practice by replacing conventional images
with images of a new and better future.*[1]

—Srivastva

Our experience in large system change suggests that incorporating the notion of community as an integral part of an
enhanced image of the modern corporation provides leaders
with an exciting opportunity to contribute to a "new tradition in
business." The tradition of community has rich roots in Western
society.[2] We believe it is a tradition that can serve to strengthen
the performance of modern organizations, the individual lives
and health of their members, and the fabric of the larger society
within which business finds its home.

The Power of Positive Images

There is an increasing body of research from a variety of
fields that suggests that our inner mental images shape our

131

outer behavior and levels of performance.[3] Larry Wilson, author of the book *Changing the Game*, asserts that "doing things differently is a result of seeing things differently." Charles Garfield's research on peak performance in business, as well as Olympic training with Western and Soviet athletes, links positive imagery to outstanding results.

We have asked senior executives and line personnel from corporations throughout the United States, Europe, and Latin America to share their images of "corporation" and "community." No matter what sector of the organizational world participates in the dialogue, the responses are surprisingly consistent. "Corporation" conjures up images of authority, bureaucracy, competition, power, and profit. "Community" consistently evokes images of democracy, diversity, cooperation, interdependence, and mutual benefit.

If this is the case, then we may want to ask ourselves if the images, associations, and feelings that are implicit in many contemporary views of the corporation are the ones we want to guide and motivate our everyday actions in today's changing world.[4] *This is not a philosophical issue, but a pragmatic one.* The answer to this question is fundamental to achieving the business results and financial returns that will ensure the survival and health of corporations in a fiercely competitive global marketplace. The models described on the following page, with some poetic license, illustrate alternative pictures of corporate life.

Of course, these models rarely exist in pure form today. However, we would like to suggest that the expanded image of the corporation reflected in the Community Model may hold more power for creating the outstanding results required to thrive in today's turbulent environment.

Modern organizations and the promise of the "good life" have separated us from traditional ties to the land, to our families, to the community, and perhaps most importantly, from the connection to our own spirit. In this process, millions of us have been cut off from our hearts' desire—to be a part of a larger community of endeavor that is worthy of our best effort.

The Corporate "Business" Model	The Corporate "Community" Model
The corporation is a well-oiled machine	The corporation is a dynamic community
Shaped like a pyramid of individual boxes	Linked by networks of interdependent teams composed of
Manned by an army of hired hands	People with diverse characteristics using all their talents and
Under the command of a Chief Executive Officer	Guided by shared purpose and quality process
With managers who execute an aggressive strategy to attack the competition and expand market share	With leaders committed to a developmental strategy of environmental scanning linked to continuous learning for improvement
In the service of maximum quarterly financial returns to the stockholders of the corporation.	In the service of maximum long-term customer satisfaction, employee and stockholder "enrichment," and the health of the larger society.

John W. Gardner, in his penetrating examination of leadership in American life, points out that when the institutions that can provide the vehicle for people's connection to "that which is larger than self" start to weaken, the people and the society begin to weaken.[5] There is overwhelming evidence that when people lose a sense of meaning and purpose in their lives, their productivity declines, their physical and emotional health becomes impaired, and their social relationships are impoverished.[6]

These developments have been unintended consequences of the Industrial Age. Nonetheless, we are becoming painfully aware of the cost of our choices. We are approaching a 50 percent divorce rate in the United States. Throughout the West, suicide rates are up. Drug and alcohol abuse have reached the point of international crisis. The United States Alcohol, Drug Abuse, and Mental Health Administration reports that the cost of emotional problems and substance abuse reached nearly $275 billion in 1988 alone.[7] Not only are the human and social costs staggering, but their impact on the corporation is *undercutting its ability to compete in the marketplace.*[8] Is this where we intended to go? We think not. Today, business is at a crossroads, faced with an unprecedented challenge:

> Built into the concept of capitalism and free enterprise, from the beginning, was the assumption that the actions of many units of individual enterprise, responding to market forces and guided by the "invisible hand" of Adam Smith, would somehow add up to desirable outcomes. But in the last decade of the 20th century it has become clear that the "invisible hand" is faltering. It depended on a consensus of overarching meaning and values which is no longer present. So business has to adopt a new tradition which it has never had throughout the entire history of capitalism. This is, as the most powerful institution on the planet, to take responsibility for the whole.

This perspective offered by Willis Harman, noted futurist and a founder of the World Business Academy, may seem like an overwhelming burden for today's corporate leader, already concerned with rising costs, intense competition, and unpredictable changes in the larger environment.

Whether it is difficult or not, modern organizations need to confront this challenge. If they do not search for ways to provide a context for meaning and community, as well as for worthwhile purpose beyond self and wealth, they may unwittingly be "killing the goose that has laid the golden egg."

Frankly, we do not believe the transformation we are considering is as complex as it may seem. If what the current research suggests is true—that "the power of positive images is not just some popular illusion or wish but is arguably a key factor in every action"—then adopting the positive image of corporation as community may become a key factor in revitalizing corporate life.[9]

What if we were to consciously choose to think of the corporation as a community and its managers as community leaders? Is it possible to create a merger between these a ently paradoxical ideas? In fact, they are actually quite co......... ible and complementary. The Swedish word for *business*, "narings liv," literally means "nourishment and life" when translated into English, and the word *corporation* refers to "any association of individuals bound together into a *corpus*, a body sharing a common purpose in a common name."[10] *Community* has the root meaning "with unity." This suggests an evocative question. What if we were to think of the Corporate Community as being "a body of people sharing a common identity and purpose, acting with unity, to provide nourishment and life both to its own stakeholders (including stockholders) and to the larger society?"

A Vision of Corporation as Community

What would such a corporate community look like? What are the principles by which it would operate? The "Merger Tale" we share below is a vehicle for stimulating further dialogue about the possibilities of designing organizations that can create a merger between the strengths of the corporation and the vitality of a healthy community. The Merger Tale is a composite creation. A fully functioning corporation-as-community does not yet exist. However, the examples of practice we describe are occurring already in corporations across the globe. The results are documented. Some parts of the story come from our collaboration with executives who are consciously using a community development approach to speed the renewal of their organizations. Other parts of this tale are drawn from the wealth of case study and anecdotal material that is accumulating in the popular press and management literature about "vanguard management."[11]

The Corporation as A Community:

A Merger Tale

It was a difficult executive meeting. The reports showed that trend lines were flattening. Nothing alarming in the short term, nothing Wall Street would notice yet, but several of the executives in the room seemed concerned.

"The international situation is shifting. Our brands are facing stiffer competition abroad as well as at home," one said.

"The consumers' needs seem to be changing as well," another added. "You know, they are more health and quality conscious than ever, and I don't know what R&D has in the pipeline that will meet that demand."

Another added, "Frankly, getting new products developed and out the door, as well as producing and delivering the ones we have already is a complex process involving a lot of departments. The whole way we are organized and managed has promoted a type of corporate arthritis. I'm an old timer and even I'm getting concerned about the bureaucracy and turfdom around here. Everyone's working independently to be the best without thinking how it all fits together to achieve our real purpose."

The one female member of the team raised a series of issues that had recently come up in the Employee Attitude Survey:

"Our employees don't think we are listening to their creative ideas, so they keep quiet. They want a piece of the action when they help us succeed. They are no longer willing to compromise their family life in return for a base salary and the knowledge that we hit the quarterly targets. They want to contribute to a purpose that has value beyond the numbers. It's a different work force than we had ten or fifteen years ago."

Another member, respected as a strategic business thinker whose ideas had paid off handsomely over the years, challenged those sitting around the conference table:

"What is our real purpose, anyway?" he asked.

That started it!

In the discussions that followed, the group re-examined their corporate purpose, which focused solely on maximum financial returns and competitive supremacy. They realized something was missing. The CEO and his executive team decided not to wait until crisis hit, but began to actively chart the appropriate role and future direction for the business. They expanded their Strategic Planning Department to include not only business and financial analysts but also specialists in organizational strategy and large-system change. Their organizational strategy specialists assisted in the design of a series of "good conversations," based on the traditional concept of the New England town meeting. The corporate community meetings focused on what kind of business approach was needed to thrive in the last decade of the 20th century. What kind of corporation would be responsive to the needs of constituencies whose support they required for their continuing success?

The senior leadership group began a series of community meetings with representation from all levels within the organization as well as with external constituencies including employees' families, government agencies, local school systems, and key stockholder groups. They soon realized that their corporation was actually like a bustling community that included not only employees and their families but hundreds of thousands of customers, suppliers, and stockholders. Like a healthy community, the company had a name and an identity as well as a diverse population tied together by an intricate web of relationships.

The leaders asked themselves, "What if we thought of ourselves as leaders of a corporate community? How would this affect our overall strategy?" Things looked very different from this perspective. A new Statement of Purpose developed, reflecting their emerging perception of themselves as corporate community leaders:

> *The purpose of our Corporate Community is to meet the needs of our customers for high-quality goods and services, to serve the needs of our employees and their families for an enhanced quality of life, and to be a responsible corporate citizen in the larger society of which we are an integral part.*

"What happened to 'competitive advantage' or 'return on investment'?" they were asked. "Profitability is only one measure of our success," they replied. "We believe that in serving this enhanced purpose, our corporation and its stockholders will be richly rewarded financially as well as in other relevant performance measures."

With their purpose clear, they identified the values they were willing to commit to—values that would serve to guide decision making and daily behavior at all levels. The acronym I STATE was used to help people remember the core values:

I ntegrity

S upport
T rust
A ccountability
T eamwork
E mpowerment

The enthusiasm spread. Employees at all levels volunteered to be members of TAQ (Take Action Quickly)Teams to speed up the transition. They brainstormed action plans and began implementation. Some of their key contributions were to:

- Develop a *Bill of Rights and Responsibilities* for members of the corporate community.

- Analyze the *business situation,* proposing creative strategies, and suggesting "stretch objectives" that were both challenging and fun.

- Understand *customers' needs* in order to create quality partnerships.

- Identify *high leverage business and organizational processes* that needed redesign or streamlining.

- Develop *clear performance standards* and a performance feedback system that supported goal setting and self-development.

- Create a performance-based *reward and recognition system* that would reinforce the I-STATE values, including incentives for intrapreneurship and profit sharing based on business results.

- Re-think the *design of the organization* to create a "human-scale architecture" of smaller-size units focused on meeting customer needs.

- Review the corporation's key *policies and procedures* to see if they were consistent with both the I-STATE values and the Bill of Rights and Responsibilities.

- Figure out how to make *continuous learning for improvement* a way of life at the company.

- Explore *leadership development* and encourage new leadership competencies based on service, coaching, and mentoring.

- Develop methods for *broad information sharing and communication* about business issues, financial results, and other dimensions of corporate community life.

- Understand *diversity* and honor individual contribution while encouraging an environment of teamwork.

- Create a *corporate responsibility* policy and recommend projects that would benefit the health, education, and welfare of company employees, their families, the larger community, and the environment.

What began to happen was fascinating. Decades of pent-up energy began to be released, tentatively at first. Employees at all levels wondered, "Do they really mean it? What will happen if for some reason the numbers go south for a quarter or two? Is our management in this for the long haul? Will my job be affected?" People were scared and excited at the same time.

The CEO assured his senior group that he was in this for the long term. He made himself personally available to communicate this message broadly. He used the "old paradigm" reward system to nurture the "new paradigm" into existence. He held his managers accountable for acting in accordance with the Statement of Purpose and I-STATE values. Management performance bonuses that year were derived in large measure from leaders' success in fostering widespread participation at all levels in the corporate community in the service of the corporate purpose.

The CEO helped get the resources (money, time, people, and technology) needed to respond to the TAQ Team recommendations and other initiatives that sprang up. While maintaining his and the Executive Team's prerogatives to define the shape and boundaries of the playing field, the coaches gave their players a great deal of room to create the plays and manage the game.

Cross-functional Community Improvement Teams were formed to work on immediate as well as longer-term challenges and opportunities. All were supported by "community organizers," employees and managers who were trained in designing meetings for results. Interactive graphics specialists, who recorded the discussions on large wall murals and flip charts, made sure that decisions, follow-up action plans, and accountabilities were clear.

Learning became the key to success. "Learning to learn" groups were started across the company. High impact leadership education was offered in the LET GO program (Leading Empowered Teams to Grow the Organization). People at all levels were supported in learning about whole systems thinking, including processes and tools for achieving Total System Quality. The firm's information systems were redesigned to enable creative problem solving and business planning at the local level. The Great Game of Business seminar helped employees learn about financial planning so they could begin to think of themselves as owner/managers of the business.

The Family Wellness and Employee Assistance Program attracted widespread participation. Company retirees joined the Caring Companion project, volunteering their time to help in the Corporate Kindergarten and to tutor and coach children at higher grade levels who were interested in being part of a college scholarship incentive program. The Loan-a-Resource project enabled executives and other employees to share their talents with local nonprofit organizations. The employees created the "Corporate Community Today" show, an interactive video program in which they shared successes in every area of community life as well as provided up-to-date information on business performance and results.

And what were the results? Here are highlights of what happened during the first three years:

- Cycle time for new product development was reduced by 40 percent.

- Productivity increased 33 percent.

- The company received the National Environmental Award for reducing plant emissions to 50 percent less than the required government standards.

- The accident rate was reduced by 50 percent.

- After the new Corporate Kindergarten started, absenteeism declined by 30 percent, and the employee turnover rate dropped almost 10 percent.

- Divisions that instituted Wellness and Employee Assistance programs for employees and their families paid 30-60 percent less in health care costs than those that chose not to participate.

- Customer complaints were reduced by more than 60 percent.

What about the bottom line? The above statistics begin to hint at what occurred. Since the corporate community development process began, operating profits more than doubled and they are still breaking records.

Change itself is hard, and not without its critics. The corporation has had to be sensitive to those who argue that, in serving as a catalyst for the re-creation of community in people's lives, it is returning to the paternalism of an earlier age clothed in new garments. It has needed to balance the universal needs for individual achievement with those for joint effort—the desire to stand out while staying in. It has had to meet the formidable challenges of nurturing shared culture and values in a community that is not geographically based. It has struggled with how to design integrated systems, processes, and structures consistent with its purpose and values, while at the same time remaining flexible and responsive. Even with all these

141

dilemmas, the corporate community continues its journey because its people have decided that the destination is worth the trip.

The elected employee representative to the Board of Directors summed it all up when he was asked why the employees had become such committed partners in creating a positive future and in sustaining outstanding results. He paused for a moment and then commented thoughtfully, "You know, I think it's because we are becoming value-led rather than market-driven."

The Role of Leadership

The role of leadership is critically important in facilitating the transition described in "The Merger Tale" we have just told. We have been working for several years with Mike Szymanczyk, a senior executive who has held key positions with several large multinational consumer products corporations, including Procter & Gamble, Kraft General Foods, and Philip Morris U.S.A. With him and other key leaders in these companies, we have explored the conscious use of community development approaches as the basis for long-term systemic change. We interviewed Mike regarding why he has used the community development model in preference to the traditional business development model and what he sees as the role of the leader in this new type of organization.

Whole Systems Associates (WSA): Why do you think that the image of community is important to use?

Mike Szymanczyk (MS): Because it gets results.

WSA: But why does it get results?

MS: I think it gets wider utilization of the talent that's in the organization. Together with our people we are getting more focus and effort applied toward common goals, and, therefore, we get a better result. It tends to keep people more self-sufficient and less needy. In the traditional business model they're needy because they're not being fulfilled.

WSA: Are they more fulfilled in the community model?

MS: What happens in a community that's well functioning is that the people in it provide for their own needs, either individually or collectively. The objective is to create an organization that has a higher level of comfortableness with itself, the way it's existing, what it's doing, how it's growing, and how it's feeling about itself. Therefore, it can spend more of its time, focus, and energy on accomplishing its common goals. It becomes a self-fulfilling prophecy.

WSA: How is the community model different from the business model?

MS: Most business models are highly competitive models. Basically people are working their own agenda in an effort to succeed in this competition against the criteria that management at the top has set up. Some of that is productive to the business and a bunch of it isn't. The community model starts from a different place. The community has a purpose rather than a criteria. And that purpose is decided on by the whole of the community and not just the people at the top. The community generally gets dissatisfied with the people at the top having a purpose that's different than theirs.

WSA: Because community leaders are, in a sense, the representatives of the people.

MS: Right. So they have a purpose that is of the whole and they work to serve that purpose. Rather than the people serving a master, even a benevolent master, they are serving a common purpose and they have the freedom to pursue their purpose. The community is organized in teams or groups who feel accountable for doing their share. The whole effort rises on the basis of their energy and achievement. Their life is better both in terms of overall quality and short-term rewards if they are productive members. So, to me, the community model is a systemic approach driven by the whole, and the traditional business model is a more segmented approach, driven by a few. It's a major structural difference.

143

WSA: The question is who should decide the purpose.

MS: If it is the leadership and if the purpose they're going to decide on is not consistent with the values and needs of the employees, there is a problem. It's not that the leaders are right and the employees are wrong. For example, in a leveraged buyout, management may want to sell off pieces of the company to increase short-term returns. Employees may want to build the business for the long term to provide security. These are conflicting purposes, typically based on different values. When values-based differences like this exist unresolved, the leadership has a tough job. Most of the time organizational productivity suffers and employees withdraw their commitment to the company.

WSA: What does that say about the role of the leader?

MS: Well, our primary role as leaders is to understand what our employees and the other constituencies want as their purpose. We facilitate communication, including listening. We are also connectors between all the various constituencies and the key connection is the discovery of shared purpose. Leaders should question how progress toward the purpose is going. Our job as senior executives is to remove obstacles by seeing that structures and decision processes are well-aligned with the company's purpose. If the purpose is right and the structures and processes that allow the connection to the purpose are right, it'll work and it doesn't matter how big it gets.

WSA: And if you were going to use the fundamental assumptions of a community development approach to make a massive change in a big system, what would you do as a leader?

MS: You'd do a lot of work to understand what people wanted as a common purpose, not only among the employee base but among others who are a part of the picture. And you'd look for commonalities. The dilemma is when you have a conflict of purpose, for example, between the employees and the shareholders like I described before in the leveraged buyout example. Whose company is it, anyway? That's what it comes down to. The fact is that it's the shareholders company. They own it. The hardest situation is the one where there's black and white between the employee base and what the shareholders want. So the solution is to help employees become shareholders so they can also have ownership in the company.

WSA: Is that different in a community?

MS: You never have that dilemma in a healthy community because, in a sense, the community is owned by the whole. Everyone is a shareholder. So when a community is planning its future, the leaders might say to its "shareholders," "Hey, we've all agreed we want a church; we want the streets to be safe; and we don't want to pay too much in taxes, but we want to pay enough to have these services. Now, here's the current situation. Our streets aren't safe. Our church is old. Our taxes don't pay our bills. Here's a possible game plan. People, are you comfortable with this game plan? How should we improve it?" And you have community meetings and they say, "Well I'm not comfortable with this; why don't we try that." There is no reason why a leader of a corporation can't act like the leader of a community.

WSA: So the leaders architect the community building process and ask the right questions.

MS: Right. And they gather the information; and they facilitate the communication of it. And they gather more information from that. And, ultimately, what they get is a kind of common game plan based on congruence with the basic purpose.

WSA: Do you think the excitement and positive energy you've seen in the companies you've worked with is because you're working with a different set of assumptions—the community approach?

MS: That's right.

WSA: At Whole Systems, we believe there is something about the human spirit that is very fundamental to building a strong community. There's this yearning. A fundamental hunger that is not getting fulfilled. There's never enough money to satisfy the spirit.

145

MS: No, I disagree here. I think there is never enough of anything to satisfy the spirit. I think the fundamental issue with human beings isn't "satisfy the spirit and then they'll be satisfied." It's that human beings are never satisfied. With anything. There is a fundamental curiosity in a human being about "what if. . . ." And it applies to everything. This is what's so special about human beings.

WSA: So what does that mean for the business?

MS: The business potential is this: If I keep giving you more money to satisfy you, I can never give you enough. If I keep creating the opportunity for you to explore your own potential in the exploration of the business' potential, then we have a positively reinforcing system. The opportunity of the community model is to build this reinforcing system and have people feel rewarded and satisfied and fulfilled from it instead of feeling like the only possible reward or satisfaction they can get is another raise or another bonus check. That's not to say that monetary reward systems aren't important. They're just not enough. I believe that one of the truly mystical things about the human organism is that it's always developing, just like a healthy community. There's always more. There's never an end. And that's what grows community, grows people, and grows the business at the same time.

The Creation of a Positive Future

It is our hope that exploring the image of the corporation as a community will stimulate further dialogue about this intriguing possibility. The essence of a nation's best hopes were described over three centuries ago by John Winthrop (1588–1649), one of America's founding fathers, just before landing in the Salem harbor. He described in poignant terms the "city set upon a hill" that he and his fellow pilgrims intended to found:

> We must delight in one another, make others' conditions our own, rejoice together, mourn together, labor . . . together, always having before our eyes our community as members of the same body. [12]

146

The yearning to be a part of and contribute to the common good is still alive and well throughout the world. The tradition of community has honorable roots—roots that the contemporary corporation can now help nourish in the soil of modern life. We do not believe the corporation can or should become all things to all people. However, we are convinced that business today has an unprecedented opportunity to fulfill its economic potential while also serving as a potent force for enhancing the quality of human life and the renewal of the human spirit.

Reference Notes:

1. Srivastva (1990), 116–17.
2. Bellah (1985).
3. Garfield (1986); Harman and Rheingold (1984); Progoff (1963); Srivastva (1990).
4. Morgan (1986).
5. Gardner (1990), 113.
6. Frankl (1963); Harman & Hormann (1990), 135–96; Progoff (1963).
7. *Brain Mind Bulletin* (April 1991), 8.
8. Adams (1988), 42–47.
9. Srivastva (1990), 97.
10. Trachtenberg (1982), 5.
11. For examples of "excellent practices" see Harman & Hormann (1990), 161–95; O'Toole (1985); Peters (1987); Peters & Waterman (1982); Peters & Austin (1985). For individual case studies and perspectives by company leaders see Autry (1991); DePree (1989); Parker (1990). For an exploration of alternative technology strategies see Zuboff (1988). For material on learning organizations and continuous improvement see Senge (1990); Imai (1986). For examples of corporate ethics and social responsibility see Freudberg (1986); Liebig (1990).
12. Bellah (1985), 28.

CYNTHIA F. BARNUM is the founder of Consulting Network International, Inc. in New York City. As a writer, commentator, and consultant, she specializes in globalization and its effects in both the media and the business world. She has lived and worked for over twenty years in seven different countries and speaks English, Arabic, French, and Spanish. Ms. Barnum's background includes a variety of roles: writer and journalist on the foreign desk at CBS News, liaison between Mobil Oil Company and the Saudi Arabian government, cross-cultural facilitator at IBM's European headquarters in Paris, and staff/consultant/master trainer for Moran, Stahl & Boyer, Inc.

Her column, "Global Mirror," appears bimonthly in the *International Executive* magazine. She also created and edits the newsletter *PARADIGM 2000* on work force diversity and globalization. She has helped to found the Diversity Management Association and is a frequent public speaker. She is currently working on a book, *Becoming a Global Citizen* and a television talk show, *A Global Conversation*.

10

Effective Membership in the Global Business Community

Cynthia F. Barnum

Today we need global cooperation to get things done, and we're faced with the need to work together on tasks that affect the welfare of those who live half a world away, as well as ourselves. But we were never trained to do this, and we're faced with each other's foibles as never before. Thanks to the Information Age and our global communication networks, there's no excuse anymore for our shocking ignorance about the world as a whole and each other as individuals. We simply cannot afford not to know. But, how do we begin? And what do we need to know and do differently now that we all live in the same global neighborhood?

In business the problems are especially acute. Despite the fact that our economy was the first man-made system to *go global*, most managers are still in the Dark Ages when it comes to knowing about their global customers, their options, or the competition. From the buying habits of the Argentinians to the negotiating styles of the Japanese, it's kindergarten out there. A recent study revealed that 70 percent of American managers admit to having "little or no experience dealing with *Americans* from different ethnic backgrounds" let alone dealing with other-than-Americans! No wonder the failure rate of our international joint ventures is 43 percent and climbing, according to a new Columbia University Business School survey. The average lifespan of our joint ventures is 3.5 years, when we are up against competitors like Toshiba who have a 250-year corporate plan!

We have little exposure to and little experience working with our differences in successful ways. But, we're already living in a "borderless world" of business and finance, as described by Kenichi Omhae, in his book of the same title. This Japanese partner of the global McKinsey and Company consulting firm is a good example of the power and potential of global synergy, where things have progressed way beyond "coping" with differences and become a matter of competitive edge. The point is to leverage and thrive on differences, not just to cope. But how do we get from here to there? How can we learn to reap the benefits of our diversity? And is there a cost-effective way to teach this? How can we train ourselves to become global and multicultural, so that we are fully capable of doing more than one job, in more than one language, in more than one country at a time?

In a 1990 memo to CNN staff members, Ted Turner stated his belief that there are no foreigners in a global world. He challenged his people to see the world, each other, and themselves in a way that makes sense to his global operations. His correspondents, like Peter Arnett in Baghdad during the Gulf War, might take the heat when global and national interests seem to conflict, but that's the whole point. This paradigm shift we sum up with the word globalization has all kinds of ramifications, but the bottom line is still the interface between beliefs and power. As a critical mass of the population takes on a new belief, the map of power changes.

Turner's idea is powerful because it puts a new belief to work. That is how you change the way people think and act. It is also the way people change the world, as Turner has done with his Cable News Network. What made CNN global? The fact that it is a twenty-four-hour show, just like the world is, only Turner saw that ten years before most people did. He was also smart and dogged enough to turn that realization into real money. He saw the positive aspects when most others were seeing only negatives, like the "threat" of global competition and the "threat" of Japanese imports. Ten years from now, where will Turner and CNN be? More importantly, where will you and your company be?

Getting a Global Mentality

Most people can't even define the word globalization adequately, much less turn a profit from it like Turner has, but that will change. Many have already realized that the whole world ought to be viewed as a single market, but that has yet to change the way they do business. You can tell right away whether or not corporate people have this global mentality. Those who have it behave and think differently from others who are working with only a local/national mind-set. For instance, you can tell they are global when "they talk about a 150-hour work week spread out over fourteen time zones," says Franck de Chambeau, director of Corporate Effectiveness for Aetna.

Other clues are likely to come from their *global vocabulary*. At the 3M company, Arlan L. Tietel talks about *global work force diversity*. And Zurich-based Asea Brown Boveri's pioneering CEO Percy Barnevik talks about how to build a "multi-domestic enterprise" that leverages core technologies and global economies of scale without eroding local market presence and responsiveness. He says, "We are a federation of national companies, with a global coordination center. We are not homeless. We have many homes."

But it all begins with the individual and what he or she believes about the world, each other, and themselves. To grow a global mentality, you have to begin with the core of the personal value and belief system. After twenty years living and working in seven different countries myself, I can tell you that global is too big, too overwhelming, and too long term to do unless it can be internalized and integrated at the most intimate level. And unless the core belief system of the individual is engaged, no lasting changes will come about, and the momentum demanded by the global learning curve will not be maintained.

Most of us already know that every action we take is being motivated by our core set of values and beliefs, even though it would be hard for us to actually sit down and make a list of them. But that's the point, and that's the level we must deal with if we want genuine effectiveness to result. The aim is global respond-ability. There is a virtual explosion in global business opportunities today but most people aren't able to capitalize on them because they haven't the vision, the skills, or the capacity to act decisively in a global way. Are you ready, able, and willing to do what you do anytime, anywhere, with anyone? Could you work effectively with a Japanese boss or a French one? Could you keep a truly global team on track? Or are you surrounded by people who all speak the same language, have the same skin color, and know only one national anthem?

By changing just one belief, a whole cascade of other changes can be set into motion. You'll never learn French, for instance, unless you are convinced that it is vitally important. The same is true for learning the *global language* and getting a *global education*. You must first be convinced that it is of vital importance. And because globalization requires a commitment that won't quit, it must become part of you, part of your belief and value system. To do this you have to *personally internalize* the global experience in a powerful way. Doing this will affect your most intimately held beliefs, but only you have the power to decide what's important at that core level. Unless globalization means something to this inner part of you, you will never become sufficiently motivated to acquire new attitudes, new skills, and the knowledge necessary to profit personally and professionally from globalization.

Going Global from the Inside Out

In order to attain effective membership in the global business community, there are some prerequisites:

152

- You need to recognize that this global community already exists.
- You have to decide you want to join it.
- You have to commit yourself to the adaptation process.
- You have to learn the global business culture.

This is a lot like moving to a new country and learning another language for those of you who have already done that. The global business community is just like any other community, only it's newer and more complex. It has a particular set of values, attitudes, and behaviors that distinguish its members from any purely local or national culture. There is a shared sense of belonging, which comes from a common set of experiences, concerns, relationships, and knowledge. This is also true at the level of corporate cultures and is very evident to anyone leaving one company and trying to become an" insider" at another one.

The members of the global business community can recognize each other. For one, they speak the same global language, no matter whether it's being expressed in Japanese, German, Arabic, or English. They are in touch with global news and events and their priorities are global. They've internalized a global education, and their experiences qualify them for the respect they receive from their fellow members, be they people in the same field or the same industry.

The Foundation

Awareness of global interconnectedness is the key. Most globally aware individuals can tell you about the gradual process they experienced or the "ah-ha" moment when they suddenly realized "it's all one world." From Earth Day to the Amazonian rain forest, it may have been their interest in ecology and the environment; for others it may have been actual travels, or exposure to international organizations like the United Nations or humanitarian relief agencies, even the Peace Corps. Space exploration has also contributed to the "one world" realization, as indicated by astronomer/scientist Carl Sagan during the twentieth anniversary of the moon walk when he commented, "Getting to the moon was perhaps not as important as seeing ourselves from it."

Whatever the source, being able to think and feel interconnected on a global level is what's causing the paradigm shift here. The world *is* borderless when seen from a high enough perspective, and this has all kinds of implications: socially, politically, economically, and even spiritually, as we are learning. Regardless of how the awareness began, it generally culminates in a sense of *global citizenship* that may be articulated in various ways.

This new appreciation of our interdependence can be extremely useful in business. (It can also be extremely dangerous when it's ignored.)

Globalization demands that individuals develop a sense of comfort that will allow them to be effective "anywhere, any time, with anyone." It's imperative that you can see the connection, literally. The aim isn't to learn everything about every country—that would be impossible. The best approach is to develop a sense that "I belong anywhere I am, no matter who I am," as Barbara Walker, international diversity manager at the Digital Equipment Corporation explains to her people. "This will allow people to feel safe enough to pay attention to differences and feel confident enough to take risks," she adds. Since Digital operates in sixty-four countries, this makes sense. It's not the point to know all the specifics of all those cultures, it's the *attitude* about them that counts more.

A Global Passport?

When you become a global citizen on the inside, your external identity begins to expand to accommodate this new belief. This is true for organizations as well as individuals. You can be both a global citizen and a patriot with a strong sense of local and national identity. But, you will have to mediate the conflicts of interest that this may cause.

After you've given yourself global citizenship, you must extend this right to *all others without exception. We are all global citizens.* What differs between us is actually only our level of awareness about this. The global "club" is open to all. *Inclusivity* is the critical value here. Your global effectiveness will be hindered in direct proportion to the degree of exclusivity you practice. By this I mean that outright prejudice and racism have no place here. If you wish to be accepted as a credible business colleague, then you must begin by extending that same courtesy. Global managers know how to relate to individuals, and not to get bogged down in old stereotypes. They know better than to write off whole categories of people on the basis of preconceived notions about group characteristics. They don't assume that "all Spaniards are lazy," for instance, if they take a mid-day siesta. They look beyond the cultural specifics so they'll be able to distinguish the really lazy ones from the hard workers!

The result you are after is *effectiveness,* and although it may be human nature to "label" people, it's a lazy way of seeing the world. You will be hard pressed to break out of the box others may have put you into unless you've corrected your own tendency to do the same. The more global you get, the more fascinating and complex people seem to be, but this openness to individuals from all over is not automatic. To go global you must widen your personal relationships until they include people from all kinds of countries. This is accomplished *one by one,* one individual relationship at a time.

Just recognizing that other peoples' beliefs are *valid for them* will get things started off on the right foot. Nothing has the power to create bonds like the ability to communicate at the level of values and beliefs, especially when dealing across barriers of culture, language, and distance. But communicating at this level must be learned and practiced, and, it is more problematic when the parties depend on interpreters. Whenever beliefs and values are in conflict, the personal relationship must be there in order for the differences to be resolved. Since business flows over the bridges of relationships, this should come as no surprize, but what's new to many Americans is the need others have to put the affiliation ahead of the tasks. From Brazil to Saudi Arabia, the bottom line would be better served if the relationship came first. Long-term profitability depends on relations and trust. As the former U.N. Assistant Secretary General Robert Muller puts it, "To create a relationship of *trust*, 'x' and 'y' must learn each others' beliefs."

Globalization is only an abstraction unless it is brought down to the level of beliefs and values. And that is why global business people operate with an understanding of *universal values*. The global business community could not exist without them, because only they have the power to cross those cultural, racial, and ethnic barriers.

They consist of the most basic beliefs, like the need to *belong*. As Maslow and other psychologists have demonstrated, this is both basic and universal, so make use of it when motivating yourself and others. The same is true for the need to feel *effective*, a trait shared by people everywhere. When you can combine these values, and others that are important to the success of your particular business, you will have the power to generate loyalty, productivity, and a host of other behaviors, anywhere, in any language. So let's focus on how to decipher values and beliefs from attitudes and behaviors in ourselves as well as others.

Three-Step Program for Developing Global Competence

Although globalization encompasses everything from "environmental scan, competitive strategy, teams and alliances, changes and chaos, and issues of personal effectiveness," as Stephen Rhinesmith, the well-traveled consultant and former president of Holland America puts it, all these items and how we deal with them can be traced back to our core set of values and beliefs. The trick is to map those well enough to be able to use a *cultural intelligence system*. To collect, analyze, and apply complex information about differences in values and beliefs, you need to draw upon different *cultural lenses*. This will build up your capability to see yourself, others, and the world through a *global perspective*. Without this, you can not grow a global mentality and the attitudes, skills, and knowledge it brings.

Briefly, my program uses the following:

First Perspective—*Your* perceptions, of yourself, your culture, your organization, in a comprehensive manner.

Second Perspective—*Their* perspective on you and your culture, as well as their view of themselves and how to decipher the beliefs behind the behaviors.

Third Perspective—*Theirs on each other*, whether or not you are involved. This is the genuinely global perspective and requires a global team of people who not only represent the major areas of the world but who have been trained to collect, analyze, and apply cultural intelligence.

Step One: The First Perspective

"Know thyself" is imperative, and your insights about your own country can be a form of *cultural capital* that you bring along when joining the global community. The way you see yourself is culturally conditioned, just as everyone else's view is, so you begin by developing a common language for discussing what culture is. Being able to talk intelligently about a neutral subject like culture is a great way to start getting to know people who are different. As I said earlier, nothing creates bonds like being able to communicate at the level of values and beliefs, and this is how you do it.

The Iceberg Model of Culture on the following page is taken from the book by Robert Kohls, *Survival Kit for Overseas Living*. Kohls's definition of culture is a handy one for business people: "Culture is an integrated system of learned behavior patterns that are characteristic of the members of any given society. It refers to the *total way of life*. It includes everything a group of people *thinks, says, does and makes*, its systems of attitudes and feelings. Culture is learned and transmitted from generation to generation."

The wavy waterline here represents the level of awareness most people have about differences. We are usually comparing and contrasting observable actions and behaviors, "Oh, look how that Englishman is pushing the peas up on the back of his

Iceberg Model of Culture

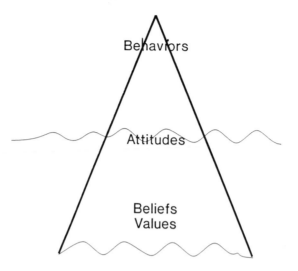

fork." But he does that because he believes and values his manners. Many Englishmen still place greater stock in formality and what's proper than in what's easier and practical, for instance. But this is only the tip of the iceberg when it comes to cross-cultural analysis. The important point is never to ignore what's under the waterline, that invisible mass of cultural preferences, myths, ideals, rituals, ceremonies, etc. What's *under* the water motivates everything above it.

To find out more about what motivates you, and others, you need to be able to construct *cultural portraits* that get at all the information not listed in a resume. To see yourself as a cultural being takes practice, but you can start with something as simple as answering the question "Who am I?" ten times, in ten different ways on a blank sheet of paper. Shoot for the bottom of the iceberg and list as many of your core beliefs and values as you can. This is what the Japanese are after when they take you out drinking in the evenings. It's an attempt to find out what makes you tick. Most of us aren't very comfortable doing this or having it done to us, but at the level of global business transactions, you must be able to do it skillfully. Values include things like independence, harmony, action, speed, and many others. Attitudes stem from deeply held values, and though we may be more accustomed to communicating at the level of attitudes, we must go deeper to penetrate cultural barriers. Here's a tool to jog your awareness.

Global Checklist for Personal Effectiveness

1. How many people can you name, in business or other fields, who have transcended their local and national origins and are considered as being genuinely global in their concerns and activities? What criteria do you use to evaluate their and your own degree of "globalness"?

2. What do your relationships reflect? Are you comfortable and credible with all nationals? Do you possess a *global mirror* or persons in your inner circle whom you trust to give you advice but who also represent the major cultures of the world? If not, then by what means do you solicit critical feedback on your performance beyond your local and national boundaries? Are you a *global negotiator*, or an American negotiating in other cultures?

3. By what system do you manage the development of your global attitudes, skills, and knowledge, and those of your key people? Have you lived/worked/traveled extensively abroad? Is your board multinational? Senior management staff, uni-cultural, or multicultural? Is your worldview helping or hindering the creation at your company of "a world to which people will want to belong," as Gilles Pajot, CEO of Pharmacutica, France, puts it in his advice to leaders.

4. Are you able to articulate the evolving *global context* your firm and your people are part of? Are they able to place themselves and their careers in that expanding global framework?

5. Do you feel excited and motivated, or fearful and threatened, by the global challenges you face? Which ones might you not be aware of? (Do you indulge in Japan-bashing, for instance, or do you look for more constructive approaches?)

6. Do you have a *global information officer?* What types of information are being collected? For what purposes? Is the

analysis and application of the data global? For instance, has your competitor intelligence unit kept pace with the global demands upon it?

7. Does the *human capital* of your organization accurately reflect the global diversity of the work force? If not, how do you expect to respond to the diversity of the global marketplace? Do you have a *designated manager of diversity*? Is it a domestic or a global job description?

8. What is the quality and quantity of the *global conversation* going on in your company? Do you "walk a global talk?" Are your people conscious of the *global profile* they have, individually or organizationally?

9. Do you and your people feel as though membership in the global business community is a daily reality?

10. Is multicultural *literacy* part of the management development process at your firm? Is there a budget for the *global education* that a critical mass of managers must have if the firm is to survive?

Lastly, what do your answers reveal about the value you've placed on all things global so far?

Step Two: The Second Perspective

Once you've dealt with the "Who Am I?", you're ready for the "Who Are They?" This question can also be answered ten different ways, at least. Choose any country and write down everything you "know" about them, using the Iceberg Model of Culture. Organize the perceptions you have according to behaviors, attitudes, and beliefs. Concentrate on what is in contrast to your own list about yourself. Having a particular national in mind makes this more useful than trying to do it in the abstract with some imaginary French person, for example. As you contemplate all things "French," think about how your own attitudes, skills and knowledge come to assist, or interfere with, the process. If you know the language and have lived in Paris for a few years, your list will look quite different from the list of someone who has never been there. That's the obvious

160

part, but the main point is, can you make a useful, objective list of French beliefs—or of the values that motivate a single Frenchman you know personally?

It takes practice to figure out what makes people tick and how to distinguish between what's culture and what's personality, but it can be done. It helps to do it with many different nationals, and to do it a lot if you want to build up your capacity for global thinking. If you find you're making too many negative judgments, then you should widen your cultural lens by consulting with someone *of that culture*. Your perspective may be limited by both your position as an outsider and the "contrast effect"—which tends to cause us to judge our ways of doing things as "right" and their ways as "wrong" when they differ. In business, there is a great advantage to the one who can see himself as others see him—that is what you should be after, *their* view of your product, your services, yourself. Consciously or unconsciously they will be using their own beliefs as the yardstick for judging you, so know how to compare those yardsticks by ferreting out their values and noting where they differ the least and most from yours. For example, if their belief in fatalism outweighs your belief in accountability, there will be conflicts down the road. This is a severe problem in the Middle East, for instance, and affects management styles in companies and even the ability to market life insurance, which is frowned upon in communities where Muslim observances are strong.

Step Three: The Third Perspective

This is where you put it all together. Now that you know how you see yourself and have some idea of how you're viewed by others (if you've solicited that information from those with a *second perspective*), you are ready to look at the "Who are we?" question. Members of the global business community are able to alternate between these points of view, informally as well as through the use of "International Diversity Advisory Boards" like the formal one set up at Digital. By using various perspectives, you will build up your cross-cultural knowledge even as you are exercising your cross-cultural communication skills. There is no better way to enhance your personal effectiveness

161

than to practice using your growing network of personal relationships with others who bring their unique cultural lenses to
the process. Most Americans might be able to tell you what they
think of the French (first perspective), but not many would be
able to tell you what the French think of them (second perspective). Still fewer could tell you how the French view the Germans and the Japanese—that's the third perspective, and the
realization of the global context.

Using this third perspective can be as simple as reading a
French magazine like *Le Point*, where a survey was held asking
French business executives to "rate" foreign executives as to
their preferences for doing business together. The French (you
may be surprised to know) put the Germans at the top of the list
(despite WWII and the Nazi occupation). The Americans came
in eighth, and the English rated ninth. Information like this has
obvious global applicability. For one, when dealing in the post-
January 1993 Europe, it might be wiser to send your German
general manager in to negotiate a joint venture in Paris than to
fly out from the United States yourself. The German will
probably strike a better deal with his French counterpart!

Most people are blithely unaware of intra-European rival-
ries, much less intra-Asian ones. But that amounts to being
globally illiterate. These days, not only should you know who
the players are, you should also be growing a capability for
operating in their arena.

To recap the use of the three perspectives, let's take something like reading up on Japan.

1. You can read something written by a fellow American.
There will be quite a range here—everything from the negative
YEN! by David Burstein to the positive, like Edward T. Halls's
new book, *Hidden Differences, Doing Business With Japan*, which
is about working with the Japanese. Some books strive to be
neutral or objective, but you also have the option of reading
works by Japanese who are naturalized Americans. Yoshi
Tsurumi, the City University of New York professor, is culturally both. He's well qualified to act as a good bridge for

Americans who want to understand Japanese and for Japanese who want to understand Americans and the interface between culture and business practices. First and second perspectives.

2. You could chose a book written from their perspective, by a Japanese citizen. A furor was created over the book *The Japan That Can Say No* by Shintaro Ishihara, because it was intended for a strictly domestic (Japanese) audience. But pirated English translations made their way across the Atlantic long before an official version did. That should have been expected in our global world! The book did some good because it was frank and critical, two things the Japanese have more difficulty being when they are with us, face to face.

3. You could choose to read a book written from a third perspective by a member of a third culture (neither Japanese nor American). An excellent example of the usefulness of this choice is exemplified by the Norwegian journalist Karel van Wolferens's *The Enigma of Japanese Power*. Seeing your subject, and your own culture, through a "third eye" like his may do more for your store of knowledge than any other volume mentioned because it's working from a more global context.

4. Lastly, you can read up on Japan's worldview by reading a book mentioned earlier, *The Borderless World*, by Kenichi Omhae. This is a genuinely global perspective!

To Sum Up

In the 1980s the global enterprise came of age. The old multinational corporation and its structure were no longer suited once more than 50 percent of revenues were being generated offshore. People back in headquarters started to see that the center was everywhere. Cross-border ownership and global capitalism are trends well beyond the scope of individual governments. Indeed, we will see the end of more than just communist regimes. Nineteen eighty-nine was a watershed year for outdated, outmoded political systems as we watched the ending of the Iron Curtain and the cracks widening in the apartheid system.

But the real test is a daily one. It all boils down to you and the way you react on the phone to someone with an accent. When you walk down the street of your home town or a global city—like New York, Paris, London, Tokyo— how do you feel? What is your level of excitement or frustration when you deal with people whose ideas and thought patterns are different from your own? Either your ethics and beliefs are evolving to keep pace with what globalization is demanding, or they are not.

Try something radical. Choose someone from the cultural or racial group with which you *have the most difficulty dealing*. Be that a white, black, Asian, Hispanic, or any other kind of American or global citizen. Try seeing them as an individual. Talk with them about culture, about their attitudes, values, and beliefs, and tell them about yours. Commit yourself to an ongoing dialogue with them, and with others. Talk about what globalization means and your definitions of it. Make that person your designated resource and facilitator. By learning to overcome your deepest prejudice, you will make the most progress in the least amount of time.

As I've said, it's by changing just one belief that we can set a whole cascade of changes into motion. And it's done one belief at a time, one individual at a time. I wish for each of you the many gifts of effective membership in the global business community.

DAVID R. GASTER is a consultant, management coach, and trainer who works principally in the United States and Europe. Born in Oxford, England, he has lived in Europe, Africa, and the Middle East. He recently retired as chairman of the PACE consulting and training group in the UK and is now a permanent resident of the United States. His background includes fifteen years in the international aviation business. For two years, he was a member of the British Aerobatic Team. He is a fellow of the Institute of Directors (UK) and a member of the British Association of Aviation Consultants and the European Federation for Management Development.

Mr. Gaster works with key executives and teams on issues of leadership and vision. His clients have included British Airways, British Telecom, IBM, ICI, The Commission of the European Communities, and the National Health Service. He is a visiting speaker at the Sundridge Park Management Centre in England, and his work has been described in *International Management* magazine and the London daily *Financial Times*.

11

A Framework for Visionary Leadership

David R. Gaster

The job of leaders is to think from their heads, communicate from their hearts and to act from their guts.

Over the past few years I have had the pleasure of working with some outstanding leaders from all levels of business. I was able to observe their ways of leading their organizations through the challenges that they faced. This chapter sets out to examine some elements of the domain in which leaders operate and to synthesize some of the patterns of their ways of leading.

I am indebted to all my teachers.

The impact of business on our world is profound and growing. High-tech aids ease daily chores; new technology opens breathtaking possibilities; brilliant marketing stimulates the "need" for new products; and the ecological networks that sustain life are being increasingly damaged. In all of this, business plays a key role. And business is alternately praised and blamed by the public, the media, and politicians, according to the focus of the moment.

Business today has great power, and, far more than government or education, it is business that is creating the culture and the society in which our children will grow up. Business has the power that knowledge bestows: the knowledge from marketing surveys, sales data, and projections. It has the power of selecting the consumer's menu: choosing which products to make and how to position and price them. It has the power of influence through advertising, promotions, and sales effort. And through size and money, the power to affect government and community decisions—whether consciously or unconsciously.

Such power demands requisite responsibility in the civilized society we pretend to be, and that responsibility rests ultimately upon the leader of each business. It is he or she who must ensure that the people in the business understand their participation in that responsibility and, crucially, *how* to discharge it. That is, how to be responsible to the larger society in which the business operates while being responsible to the business as a producer of profit.

Responsibility to society often appears as a counter-pull to business success—fighting off environmental controls will produce quicker and bigger profits; even building a solid foundation for the future will hold back next quarter results and disappoint the financial markets. Always the short term is pressing, and the need to react quickly often overshadows the need to react well. Today's enormous pressures from recession, globalization, increasing competition, changes in the work force, and concern about the environment hit the leader from all directions: shareholders, banks, employees, and customers. Given such multidimensional pressures, it's easy to lose grip on the corporate mission and the personal vision of the leader. The slide is subtle, swift, and hard to reverse.

Too often the guide becomes profit and the only real limitation is government legislation. "What is the maximum cheap fill legally allowed?" "What is the maximum over-booking?" "What is the minimum environmental compliance?" These are all issues that must be considered, but a business driven by such questions suffers a "thought virus" within its management that is more deadly than the toughest competitor.

The risk for a business in our time is that it will lose its mission in the tangle of day-to-day issues so that the guiding light becomes diffused, confused, and even abused. The excesses of the '80s, the useless mergers and acquisitions, and the junk bond financing that made it all possible were giant demonstrations of greed and short-term thinking. But each one of us has had interactions with businesses that are examples on a more human scale. These are particularly sad from corporations with mission statements that project fine values and beliefs. Indeed, such mismatches drive a wedge through the integrity of any organization by invalidating the words of the leaders.

The real opportunity for a modern business is that it can positively contribute to the creation of our society, of the culture our children will inherit, while achieving business success. It can help to create a world to which we shall all want to belong. Here then is the greatest challenge to the leader—to keep the thinking clear, to continue to testify to the vision even in the face of adversity, even in the midst of the tough, everyday grit of reality, even when it would be much more comfortable to acquiesce to short-term solutions that all around are urging.

The great leaders manage this without being torn by conflicting needs and without ruining their health in the process. The poor leaders lose their way, their momentum and their clarity; the path that their people could follow is lost as they spread their own confusion into mixed messages (e.g., "Do as I say—not as I do" or, in Argyris's terms, "Theory espoused versus theory in use"). Such tangles of mixed messages, which are often conveyed quite unconsciously in micro-behaviors, result for the leader in tension, stress, and the paradox of "trying to relax" or "demanding participation in decision making." Results for the next level down are, at the minimum, confusion, which leads to poor management and thus poor handling of corporate responsibilities—for profit and for society. We have all seen too many good businesses flounder through loss of direction.

One of the characteristics that distinguishes outstanding leaders is that they have thought deeply and seriously about the kind of business they want to be running. They have asked themselves the question: "What sets the tone of the business?" They know they need to get the numbers and the strategies as right as they can; but they have also realized that "not everything that counts can be counted and not everything that can be counted counts." They have become aware that the leader's task is to create a world to which people want to belong; that all the attention paid to details, to tasks, and to fast decisions while climbing the ranks now needs to be balanced by a much larger and longer view. They have realized that there are many factors that set the tone of the company, and many possible actions to affect it. The key to the company's sense of identity and vision is the person of the leader.

There is no formal model that can coherently answer the multidimensional and paradoxical demands of the leader's operating environment. The problems are far too complex and diverse. Yet leaders *need* coherent models with which to respond consistently and productively to pressing challenges. The only coherent model they have is themselves. Leaders who are able to operate effectively at this level are frequently described as visionary, and they consistently demonstrate three key abilities. I define these skills as:

1. The skill to develop a coherent, compelling vision

2. The skill to communicate that vision effectively, such that people are empowered to pursue it

3. The skill to manage their own performance, sensitive to context, in pursuit of the vision

The rest of this chapter will offer some suggestions for the development of these three key abilities.

Creating the vision

What quite frequently happens in physics is that, from seeing some part of the experimental situation, you get a feeling of how the general experimental situation is. That is, you get some kind of picture. Well, there should be quotation marks around the word "picture." This "picture" allows you to guess how other experiments might come out.

—W. Heisenberg

"Vision" implies imagery, and the outstanding leaders do create a world inside their heads, a vision of the future, which guides their day-to-day actions; it provides the coherent model. This is an ability that we all have but few of us employ. The vision is not an attainable end state, but rather a continuing process. There is no complete description—the patterns of our minds unfold beyond our ability to describe them—but I imagine a continuously evolving hologram. There is enough substance to make it almost tangible, yet sometimes it lurks in shadows. Sometimes it is alive with sound and brightness, and sometimes it is tranquil. But it is always connected at a deep level with the heart and with the gut.

Vision grows in the feedback-feedforward relationship between what might be (the world in the mind) and the present potential (the sensitive perception of the environment), and it thrives on difference. Indeed, vision seems ever elusive like the rainbow—wherever one moves, it is just beyond reach. Yet like the North Star, it is a powerfully reliable guide.

Since vision is systemic, it sees the parts and the whole in a way that the linear progression of words can never achieve. It can map the flow of the links of value from the heart of the business to the customer, and through the business to the stakeholders. It emphasizes the patterns that are the life of the business.

In order to build this hologram called vision, it is absolutely necessary to take a step back from the day-to-day issues. It is a qualitatively different mode of thinking than that of everyday

171

management but will produce a level of certainty that informs each management decision. Allow some quiet time in which you can really reflect in a relaxed state of mind. An easy walk in the country or a quiet evening alone provides suitable settings for most people.

Once you've established a setting or a context for reflection, think ahead to your retirement years. Imagine you are looking back to your time as a leader.

What were the accomplishments that you are most proud of?

Most of us find it easier to think in terms of business results, but much more important here is the context in which those results were achieved—the sustainable qualities that you engendered in the organization.

What was your legacy? What sort of company did it become?

What was it like to work for? To be a customer of?

These may be metaphorical notions at first. Whatever the metaphors, let them gradually develop into becoming examples of your future company. Focus on the *qualities* underlying these metaphors until the elements that are really important to you become clear. Notice, by the way, that you can manipulate the images in much the same way that you adjust the controls of a television set. You can make the image brighter or darker, clearer or blurry, moving or still, and even larger or smaller. Such adjustments help develop the vision as you become more aware of your own "envisioning process." If you think you don't have time for such thinking, please realize that the future of your company and the dignity of your retirement depend on it.

Now you have the movie. Next, we add sound. Begin to hear the quality of the voices in the interactions you imagine. They can indicate much about the quality of the relationships you see in the future company. Then make sure that your own emotions are involved in the process. What is your gut response to the images and sounds you are creating? It is critical that you include your feelings because only in that way can the vision come alive for you and shift from being just an intellectual and disassociated idea to a vision that is alive and potent.

Notice that there is a difference between watching yourself in the future scene and actually imagining being there, seeing out of your own eyes. An example may make this clearer. Imagine standing in a fairground, watching *yourself* on a roller coaster. See yourself at the top of one of the peaks. Now, switch perspective and imagine seeing your hands gripping the handhold and the track dipping away in front of you. The second "associated" perspective will typically produce much more sensation and will make the vision more real.

Wisdom has been defined as the ability to see the world from different points of view, and it is important that vision has wisdom. A single perspective can never produce a rich enough world to create a coherent model. The task is to inform the vision further by shifting perceptual position. Imagine yourself being a customer of your future company—really step into the customer's shoes and find out how you, as the customer, would respond to your imagined company. Investigate as many different perspectives as you can. Imagine being secretary, vice-president, factory worker, or service engineer. In each case you might ask, "What do I expect from my company and what does my company expect from me?" Imagine being a community neighbor of the corporation, or look from the naive wisdom of a child; it will add yet another dimension.

As a final perceptual position, ride the space shuttle and look down on your business within its community, the community within the nation, and the nation within the global system. Does your vision contribute to creating a world to which you wish to belong? Only by considering these different perspectives can the vision evolve into a form that guides the organization so that everyone's integrity is respected and, therefore, the vision is fully supported.

Vision is not plan-able, but it can be program-able; it exists in the relationship between your conscious and unconscious thoughts. It can't be rushed or made to order, but following the above steps will help to create contexts in which it can develop. You may find that the steps loop back—that an image that appeared appealing from the outside can feel quite wrong from the inside; or that information developed by shifting perceptual position leads to a review of the initial qualities. Such looping will become a continuous process, since vision is not a fixed picture but an ever-evolving process—a continuing pursuit of the elusive ideal. It is that pursuit that generates the coherent model to guide action and creates the emotional charge that is at the heart of good leadership.

Communicating the vision

The orientation of the chief executive towards internal communication was seen as the single most important factor influencing patterns of behaviour.

—From a report by the UK consulting division of Smythe Dorward Lambert following a survey of major companies entitled: "Your Employees —Your Edge in the 1990s."

Having a vision of the future implies a difference between what is now and what might be. The leader must lead by being ahead of the organization in thinking (the vision) and action (pursuing the vision). The leader who wants the organization to evolve must lead by evolving himself. All the other appropriate business moves, like restructuring, divestiture, training, and so on, will naturally occur in pursuit of the vision, and their timing and style will be illuminated by it.

As the vision becomes more real, you can begin to see differences between the kind of leader you are and the kind of leader you want to be. Self-observation is the first key. Communicate and observe your communication. By becoming more aware of the choices you make, both conscious and unconscious, you can increase the range and quality of those choices.

The great leaders create a context in which visions can be realized. They do this by communicating their own vision with conviction in such a way that the people they work with can "buy into" and become a part of it. So the vision, rather than a forced direction, becomes the coherent framework, refined and enriched by each person uniting behind it. This is a two-way process; the leader needs to read people sensitively and accurately, since much of the information he or she operates from comes secondhand.

The question is how to start. The simple answer is that the leader alone must begin by living with reference to the vision, finding out firsthand how it works in everyday activities. This is simple, but not easy. Assuming that your vision includes people who are empowered to get the job done and take care of the customer, begin by noticing how *you* get the job done and how *you* take care of your customers, both internal and external.

For example, after a meeting with one of your VPs, take a few moments to review the interaction and remember the state in which that person left your office. Were they empowered? If not, track back through the meeting and find out what disempowered them. You can only learn as you go; as Aldous Huxley said, "Experience is not what happens to you, it is what you do with what happens to you." You can develop your leadership skills by becoming aware of the process you use to communicate your leadership. Observe yourself in your office, notice the interactions that take place, and compare them with the vision.

"Nobody is going to listen to what you say," he assured me. "People are seldom interested in the actual content of a speech. They simply want to learn from your tone and gestures and expressions whether or not you are an honest man."

—Kurt Vonnegut, Jr.
From the novel *Wampeters, Foma and Granfalloons*

There is a useful way of looking at these interactions to add more precision. In every communication, there are two dimensions. We can consider the words as the *content*, with behavior providing the *context* through which we know how to interpret the words. I could say, in a friendly voice with a smile, "I have something to tell you." You might expect good news. Or, I could say it, pointing my finger at you and scowling, and you would expect the opposite. The point is that your behavior is creating the context of your leadership, generating far more influence than the words you use. Furthermore, it is behavior that defines relationship and good communication depends on good relationship. This does not mean that you have to like all the people you work with, but it is necessary that you have clear communication with them. Ambiguity starts people double guessing your intentions, or filtering the news they give you based on what they think you want to hear. Since you must have the whole truth, make that clear to them. Track your behavior. If in doubt, ask.

As you begin to pay attention at these levels to the micro-world of your leadership, you will find out a lot about the quality of the vision. Your observations will enrich and develop it and also clarify the differences between what is now and what you are trying to create. This will enable you to recognize where change is needed and develop appropriate strategies for change.

These strategies start with the individual in the business. In every interaction you have, there will be an opportunity to empower people to pursue the vision.

Consider the following diagram:

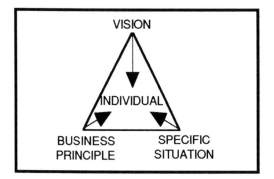

In each specific situation the individual is at center stage. With the vision as reference, use the situation to illuminate an element of the vision by explaining the business principle involved.

Such on-the-spot coaching must first pass the "need to know" versus "no need to know" filter. There's no sense explaining a complex financial principle to the janitor, but if in doubt, err on the side of talking. In a sense, leadership is a conversation. One of the finest leaders I worked with said that "leadership is not an activity but a state," and part of that "state" involves an ongoing discussion to spread the vision a little at a time. Gathering input from the people in the organization, each one the expert on his or her domain, develops the vision and tests it against the hard backdrop of reality.

Management of Personal Performance

We are capable at the same time of taking risks and estimating them beforehand. Others are brave out of ignorance. . . . But the man who can most truly be accounted brave is he who best knows the meaning of what is sweet in life and what is terrible, and then goes out undeterred to meet what is to come.

—Pericles

The outstanding leader knows when it is necessary to commit fully to a situation and how to do so. This may be a speech to motivate the troops, a negotiation with a key competitor, or an important management meeting. There are also times when it is more important to stand back, to let others carry the torch, or simply to allow time for problems to digest. Even during one management meeting it may be useful at one point to push hard, at another to pull, and at yet another to sit quietly and observe. There are two factors at play: first, the sensitivity to know which action is appropriate and second, the ability to manage one's personal performance to push, to pull, or to hold back.

The specific sensitivity that is required is sensitivity to context. This sensitivity can be a challenge to develop. Typically, in the West, it is easy enough for the leader to commit to action; it is the holding back that is difficult. Releasing direct control to others, or avoiding solving the problem until its dimensions and potentials are really understood, causes senior executives the greatest challenge. But such modes of operating are as critical at this level as is the ability to act decisively. Again, the vision will guide the leader by portraying a comprehensive view.

For a point of view to be of any use at all, one must commit oneself totally to it, one must defend it to the very death. Yet, at the same time, there is an inner voice that murmurs: "Don't take it too seriously. Hold on tightly, let go lightly."

—Peter Brook, the British film and theatre director, from the preface to his book *The Shifting Point*.

A key issue is balance. Most major decisions require multidimensional thinking between the horns of dilemma, with insufficient data and excessive responsibility. A leader needs to make good decisions; they evolve from the quality of the process of considering the problem, the outcome, and the possible solutions. Indeed one might argue that the quality of the process is more crucial than the correctness of any individual decision since the process is what is transferred to other members of the management team. It is the quality with which those decisions are made that will steer toward the vision or divert away from it. The particular challenge for the leader of the larger organization is that the evidence to be weighed must be construed from trends of data in different but interactive domains. Reliable networks must be established and the data sifted to pull out the relevant threads. Possible solutions will have multidimensional ramifications, and many imaginary worlds must be created to view the unfolding outcomes. Quality in this complex process comes from balance—physically, mentally, and emotionally.

There is a risk in developing a compelling vision and having the ability to communicate it effectively. The risk is that of being caught up by it, drawn along with it, and losing balance in pursuit of it. It may be immensely rewarding to have built a major organization, but if that is accomplished through the sacrifice of personal health or losing one's family, then what kind of reward is it? And what example does it set for others? To achieve one's best, sacrifices often have to be made, but the sacrifice of balance is never appropriate, for it is that balance that preserves the identity, the spirit, the heart of the enterprise and the core ability of living toward the vision. There have been far too many examples of unbalanced vision already.

There are times when the senior executive must operate at 100 percent and other times when it is critical to slow down; unnecessary performance, regardless of how good it is, can be as dangerous as poor performance when the best is needed. These challenges are parallel to those of athletes who need total performance at the starting gun—not two hours before or ten seconds later. For senior executives, the matter is even more important because the race has no defined ending.

The sprinter can give 100 percent because of the tape 100 meters distant. It sets a context within which full commitment can be made. The same is true of the actor during the play—the curtain falling at the conclusion denotes the context switch back to normal life. Leaders must work to create their own context markers because the business world has no clear tapes or curtains. The pressure may be on whenever the leader is in contact with the business. Modern technology provides a cellular connection almost everywhere, and modems connect the laptop to the mainframe from any hotel. The problem today is not to stay in constant contact but to find privacy; not to direct from moment to moment but to empower others to do what they do best and to guide the context of their thinking by focusing on the larger picture and the deeper trends.

Vision, communication, and personal performance. They interlock and interact, each a dimension of leadership. They set the tone for the management team and for the sense of identity of the business. Developed and integrated, they can elegantly adjust the points of greatest leverage in the organization.

For who looking dispassionately at the human race from Cro-Magnon to Auschwitz to the Gulag Archipelago can doubt that we are technological giants yet ethical pygmies.

—Charles Hampden-Turner

Technology has raced to the point where human frailty—like forgetfulness, confusion, and all our powerful emotions—can endanger our very existence. Business today can produce quantities and qualities of products undreamed of even a generation ago. But the starting point is always people—people who create, communicate, initiate, and manage the ideas that are the basis of the organization. It is the critical responsibility of the leader to manage those people with a coherent vision, which respects the integrity of all concerned and of the larger context within which it's embedded. Only in this way can we benefit over the longer term from the advances of technology rather than become slaves to institutionalized incompetence and inhumanity.

> *I think that only daring speculation can lead us further and not accumulation of facts.*

> —A. Einstein

Today's visionary leaders need guts, intellect, and skill just as in the past; and to hone their own "human" resources into vitally efficient, well-managed operating systems of high personal integrity. Take time to step back from the business, look at the larger picture, consider your legacy, and take a quiet stroll with no agenda. Allow the agenda of agendas to unfold. We are creating our future anyway.

Shall we create a future we will like?

CHARLES F. KIEFER is founder and chairman of Innovation Associates, Inc., a Boston-based consulting and training firm now specializing in enabling organizations to proactively create their future. In addition to his fifteen years of consulting experience in the areas of management of technical and professional staff and the management of technological innovation, Mr. Kiefer has held administrative and research positions at Massachusetts Institute of Technology and served on the administrative staff of the United States Senate. He founded Innovation Associates in 1976.

Innovation Associates has developed Leadership & Mastery, a novel and highly regarded course in visionary leadership for senior executives and high-potential managers, as well as related programs for building outstandingly productive and inspired organizations. Mr. Kiefer is a graduate of MIT in physics and management. He has lectured widely throughout the United States and Canada.

12

Leadership In Metanoic Organizations

Charles F. Kiefer

Today a significant shift of worldview is occurring in certain parts of our society. On a personal level, people are realizing that they are a force of nature and essentially free to create their lives however they want them to be. Certain organizations are beginning to extrapolate this point of view to realize the extraordinary power of a group of people who, securely rooted in their individual creative power, bond together to collectively bring into being a vision that none could accomplish alone.

We have termed such an organization "metanoic." Metanoia is a Greek word meaning fundamental change in the way one thinks about life. A metanoic organization is one that has undergone a fundamental shift of orientation from the individual and collective belief that people must cope with life and, in the extreme, are helpless and powerless, to the conviction that they are individually and collectively empowered to create their future and shape their destiny. In a metanoic organization people help to create the collective vision, not merely to make money but because it is consistent with their own life's purpose. Consequently, the vision held in a metanoic organization is worthy of each member's highest personal ideals and commitment.

The leadership required to bring a metanoic organization into existence is of a special quality. All great leaders stand for something. They have defined some value, issue or purpose to be of overriding importance to them. For Martin Luther King, Jr., it was freedom and civil rights. For John F. Kennedy, it was democracy and America's destiny. For Gandhi, it was freedom in India. Each of these men embodied a strong commitment to his vision. His life spirit was involved in it. Because of their commitment, others were willing to commit themselves under the leadership of these men.

In a metanoic organization, the essence of leadership stems from the leader's soul rather than from his or her behavior. There are some managers in whose presence people grow and flourish, and others in whose presence people seem to wither and die. We have all seen examples of both kinds of managers, yet some of both kinds behave like autocrats, while others of both kinds are permissive and participative. Great leadership is not primarily a function of behavior and technique. It is the commitment of leaders that inspires others, and no amount of behavioral technique will substitute for the genuine commitment of leaders to their vision.

Areas of Metanoic Leadership

The inability to *cocreate* a collectively chosen vision is perhaps the weakest link in even our very best organizations. Our organizations are populated at senior levels by leaders who can be very masterful personally; that is, when the realization of their vision is dependent *solely on themselves*, they easily create what they want. However, when the vision involves mobilizing the committed union of numerous other people, this mastery declines dramatically.

For example, most executives would have no doubt about their ability to do an excellent job creating a report for which they possess all the necessary information. But if that report involved the coordinated efforts of the several people on their immediate staff, their level of confidence might wane a bit. And if the task involved the implementation of a five-year strategic plan that required the coordinated efforts of ten thousand people, they may have little or no certainty as to the outcome. A metanoic organization calls for leaders who have developed themselves beyond personal mastery to organizational mastery; that is, they have the ability to sustain a collective vision and work in union with others to bring it about.

Leadership in a metanoic organization functions principally in three areas. First, the *leader is the custodian or steward of the organizational vision*. The leader sees to it that the organization has a collective vision and that the members share that vision and are committed to it.

Second, *the leader empowers and coaches others to create what they want;* that is, to be true to themselves and to expend their life energy creating results worthy of their human spirit. Third, *the leader is a creator of structure*. The leader maintains and shapes structures that channel the creative energy of everyone toward producing the results to which they are all committed.

These three leadership functions, while critical in a metanoic organization, have been much less important and obvious to leaders in the past. Only recently are leaders beginning to focus on creating a truly collective vision to which everyone can wholeheartedly commit themselves and putting a priority on empowering members to create the results that they as individuals want to create. Very few executives have experience working with the often unnoticed elements of structure, such as beliefs and values, which are central in focusing and unifying human energy.

Custodian of the Organizational Vision

Unlike an individual vision, an organizational vision effectively involves every member. Instead of answering the individual question, "What do I want?" it answers the organizational question, "What do *we* want?" A compelling organizational vision is vital to a metanoic organization.

An organizational vision, as the term is used in a metanoic organization, refers to a mental image of desired tangible results. Ideally, the vision is held by all members of the organization. For most organizations, their vision will be multifaceted and may include business goals but usually will go beyond them to embody noble and lofty qualities, such as a work environment where people flourish, products of superior quality, outstanding financial results, customers who are grateful and thrilled at the company's product, and so on. Each of these elements of the vision represents a definable state that could be achieved; and if it were achieved, you would know it.

The organizational creative process, however, usually begins with a number of individuals, perhaps at different levels in the organization, having personal visions of results they want to accomplish in their personal lives and in their jobs. One major challenge of the metanoic leader is to help weave the many threads of individual vision into a collective fabric that is satisfying to everyone's personal vision.

The process can begin by eliciting personal visions, welcoming any individual's attempt to formulate a vision for themselves, no matter how unclear or superficial. With encouragement, individuals can quickly reach deeper and more significant levels of vision. As this process continues, members' images of their ideal organizational life will begin to emerge. At first, they may see this only in terms of their own personal workspace and output. But if organizational imaging is encouraged, people naturally begin to create pictures of what they would like to see manifested in the whole organization. As they listen to each other's individual visions for the organization, members get their first sense of an organizational vision, and everyone becomes aware of the kind of vision they ought to develop collectively. By continuing to refine, clarify, and enrich these individual visions, a full and complete organizational vision will begin to emerge.

186

People often expect their leaders to define the organizational vision for them. And, in fact, it was historically conceived to be the job of the leader to establish the organization's vision unilaterally, obtain the commitment of the members to it, and courageously hold themselves and others to that vision, no matter what. This practice may be better than the all too prevalent coping-with-current-problems orientation, but it still falls short of what is possible. It also has some inherent weaknesses.

First, when the leader is the sole creator of the organizational vision, the members' own ability to envision the future atrophies, and they grow ever more dependent on that leader. When the leader departs, the organization is usually left with key players who lack the ability to create new visions of the future.

Second, to the extent that the vision established by a single leader is fixed and immovable, it effectively eliminates any significant degree of choice, ownership, or initiative on the part of the individual members. Given the differences among us as individuals, it is unlikely that we will ever find our vision completely embodied in another's. Accepting another's vision as if it were our own compromises what *we* truly want and results in a shallow commitment compared to what it is possible to obtain. Faced with an immovable organizational vision, members can either adopt the vision as presented (sacrificing a part of their own vision), live in compromise, or leave. In no case does the leader gain full commitment from the members. In fact, a more likely occurrence is that people will feel manipulated by the power of the leader's vision and may even, at an unconscious or conscious level, spontaneously resist it.

Regarding organizational visions, a new alternative has emerged for metanoic leaders. Their function is not to establish the vision, but to *catalyze visioning* among members of the organization. Recognizing that clarity and power of vision can come from the creative output of any individual, it becomes the leader's responsibility to ensure *that everybody in the organization is envisioning their personal future as well as that of the organization.*

A metanoic organization is managed in a way that fosters rather than suppresses the creative arguments that may surface.

In a metanoic organization, each person's vision for the organization can be as vital as any other's, because it is in the differences of these visions as well as their similarities that the underlying purpose of the organization is clarified. Since each person's contribution is vital to that clarity, each person participates in the leadership of the organization, whether or not they occupy formal leadership roles. In this process they can experience a level of responsibility and ownership in the organization as deep as any of the formal leaders. The desired state of alignment is one in which people can freely commit their life energy to a certain collectively desired result (an organizational vision). It is a state in which individuals realize that the actions they desire to take will allow them to be true to themselves as well as to their organization.

In a metanoic organization, then, the leader is primarily a catalyst of the collective vision. The leader acts as a channel for the expression of that vision. It is as if the organizational vision flows through the leadership rather than originates from it. Thus, the leader's custodial role is, first, to see that a genuine organizational vision emerges and, second, to make sure it remains alive and well.

Empowering and Enrolling People

The second major function of leadership in a metanoic organization is to enable others to come into the full presence of their own creative power. The essence of personal power is to be able to see clearly what you want to create and then habitually mobilize your resources to manifest that vision. When empowering others, the leader's task is to help them determine what is truly important for *them* and the results they will commit themselves to bring into being. This amounts to enrolling them in their own personal vision—not "selling" them, but simply allowing them to "place their own name on a roll" in favor of themselves and their vision. This state of enrollment evokes a far greater sense of personal responsibility for and commitment to a result than merely being "sold" a vision.

Most people in organizations find themselves in the position of complying with the wishes of others, particularly their superiors. Compliance does produce results; it is a proven and effective management strategy. Yet it pales in potency compared to the commitment accompanying true enrollment. There is a profound difference between doing something because *you* want to and doing something to fulfill the expectations of another. With the former, you bring an entirely different energy to the activity, a true creative energy.

In most organizations the best you hope for, and often the only thing that can exist, is compliance. In metanoic organizations this is known to be inadequate. Even so, the achievement of enrollment is made difficult by people's habit of complying, a habit acquired through years of practice as we grew up. Often compliance appears so sincere that we allow it to pass for genuine enrollment. But we really do know the difference in ourselves and others.

At the collective level, it is the function of leadership to evoke members' enrollment in the organization's vision and thus elicit from them far greater commitment, personal responsibility, and ownership of the organizational vision than could be attained by any form of "selling."

In essence, enrolling people merely involves painting a vivid mental picture of the vision for yourself and for them. You thereby make your vision available to them and allow them to sign up for it. This stance requires that you have a relationship of trust and truthfulness with them, that you are on the level with them, and are willing to let the chips fall where they may. If the vision captures their spirit, they will enroll themselves. If not, they won't.

Evoking creative potential from people and calling them to personal mastery involves continually and gently coaching them to clarify the results they truly want and encouraging them to mobilize their resources to pursue those results. This metanoic approach is in contrast to other approaches to staff development. A common presupposition of other methods is that subordinates lack certain qualities (such as responsibility, commitment, dedication, determination, motivation, and perseverance) and that leaders must do or add something to them to make these qualities grow. Such activity often involves manipulation, which diminishes a person's power, no matter how well-intentioned the activity may be. Coaching people to create what *they* truly desire is inherently non-manipulative because, at any moment in time, the power remains in the hands of the individual being coached.

One of the most revolutionary aspects of metanoic leadership is to encourage individuals to have their own personal visions, to enroll them in these visions, and to coach them in creating what they really want. The suggestions offered earlier for leaders to help catalyze visioning also work well in fostering enrollment.

In many companies it can be presupposed that the members are unaligned and that they do not share the same common interests. Thus, the metanoic approach would be potentially destructive of orderly organizational functioning. The belief is that, left to their own devices—or creativity—people would pursue irreconcilably different goals. Everyone would have their own idea of what the organization ought to be doing. Under such conditions, leaders usually see manipulation and coercion as unfortunate but necessary to keep people focused on a common objective.

In metanoic organizations leaders create an environment for alignment by evoking from the members a collective vision to which they can all be committed. The state of organizational alignment is one in which members operate as a whole, knowing that the actions taken will allow each of them to be true to themselves as well as to the organization. They see that the purpose and vision of the organization is worthy of the commitment of their life-spirit. And they, in effect, expand their definition of self to enjoy a sense of unity with every other person in the organization.

In service to that collective vision, alignment among the members naturally occurs. Alignment is a natural by-product of a group of people striving together to achieve a lofty vision. It happens when people are focused on a common objective that they also see as in some way fulfilling their own personal visions. In an aligned organization, any attempt to use manipulation or coercion would be resisted, because people are already focused on a collective goal that includes their own best personal interest.

The fact is, no one can lead an unaligned organization. In such a case, power must be used to gain compliance. Inasmuch as the members do not share a common goal and, left on their own, would pursue divergent objectives, a leader must wield power and authority in an *attempt* to reconcile these conflicting desires. But alignment will not be coerced; nor can it be created directly. Many organizations attempt to create alignment by designing ways to get people to work together, in the hope that they will then be able to achieve corporate goals more effectively. This rarely, if ever, works because people cannot commit their energy to a compromise or, particularly, to something that falls short of allowing them to express their personal life-purpose.

Creating Structure

The third principal role of a leader in a metanoic organization is to create structures conducive to creating desired results. The structure of an organization channels organizational energy in the same way that your body and mind channel your personal energy. For example, the structure of the human body predetermines the range of its possible movements. Thus, the lower leg can swing backward but not forward; the fingers can be folded toward the palm, but not away from it. So, although a person's exact physical movements may not be predictable in advance, the general character of the body's movements can. In a similar way, structure largely predetermines organizational behavior and performance and is, therefore, very important, since poorly designed organizational structure will tend to limit energy flow among members and thwart inspiration.

191

Unfortunately, a well-designed structure will not *cause* a free flow of energy or inspired performance. The most perfectly designed structure can only foster these results. The cause of inspired performance is to be found in the domain of vision and purpose.

Aligned, personally masterful individuals not only create directly what they want, they also create personal structures that are conducive to creating these results. In other words, when individuals have a vision of something they want to create, they self-consciously channel their life-force toward accomplishing that result. Simultaneously, they *create structure* which also channels their life-force toward that vision and reinforces its momentum. Leaders, however, not only create as individuals by building structures that channel their personal energy toward their visions, they also create structures that channel the energy of *everyone* toward producing the results to which they are all committed.

Symbolically, structures are like the walls and corridors of a building that govern the flow of human movement through that building. From the perspective of energy flow, structures can be treated as stationary, since they either do not change or change much less rapidly than people's actions and behavior. There are numerous structural relationships at work in organizations, the most familiar of which are those that *control* human energy. Control structures usually originate from management's desire to see that members are doing their proper tasks to best carry out the assumed purpose of the organization.

Most prominent among these control-oriented structures is the organizational *hierarchy of reporting relationships*. In this structure, energy is channeled and controlled from superiors to subordinates. Most corporations operate in such a structure, with the seniors clearly responsible for what happens to the organization and the rest of the members simply accountable to those who stand above them in the hierarchy.

But there are other control-oriented structures in organizations, which are at least as powerful, if not more so, than the hierarchy. The structure of *rewards* and *incentives*, such as compensation and performance-review systems, is one of these. People will work or channel their energy toward what they are rewarded for or paid to do. If we all agree to the value of a certain objective, yet get paid for accomplishing something else, we are most likely to produce the results that get rewarded. For example, suppose that management and sales staff alike all want customer satisfaction to be their most important objective, yet salespersons are commissioned according to the number of closed sales they make. The creative energy in this structure will flow so that there will be numerous closed sales, but perhaps not as many satisfied customers.

Besides hierarchy and rewards, there are numerous other structural elements. One such area, usually recognized as vitally important but not thought of as structural, is that of personal and organizational *goals*. Having a goal sets up a discrepancy between what we want (our vision, or goal) and what we now have (our current reality). This discrepancy generates a creative tension such that human energy is clearly channeled to move current reality toward our goal. Organizations (and individuals) usually have many major as well as subordinate goals toward which they are striving and expending energy. At times, these goals may even contradict one another and seemingly confuse and defeat energy flow. Ways for organizations to creatively utilize and profit from such apparent conflict will be suggested later.

Other powerful structures—less obvious than goals and frequently not capitalized upon by executives—also influence organizations to achieve what they want. The first of these is *belief structures*. Beliefs are those deeply held, often unconscious assumptions about the way life is or ought to be, and they tend to have a dominant influence on how people channel their energies, since people tend to behave in ways consistent with their beliefs. Strong beliefs function much like self-fulfilling prophecies. For example, if I believed people were basically dishonest and out to cheat me whenever they could, I would probably, if unconsciously, act in ways that actually provoked those behaviors in others. Over time, I would be likely to collect evidence to support that belief and in this way, my beliefs, in a very real sense, would create the reality that I experienced on a daily basis. It is unlikely I would expend my creative energies in directions I believed to be untrue, wrong, bad, or impossible. On the other hand, beliefs consistent with what I want can be enormously helpful in channeling creative energies. A desirable belief might take the form, "People are basically capable, trustworthy, dependable, etc."

Other often overlooked powerful structures for channeling energy are *values*: the qualities of life we care most about, such as freedom, truth, health, happiness, and the like. Whether we inherit our values or choose them, we direct our energies, subconsciously even more than consciously to their expression and accomplishment. So values too, are paths along which an individual's creative energies naturally flow. In any organization, the values held collectively by the members tend to function in the same way, creating a path along which everyone's energies seem to flow.

Habits are another neglected set of structures. At the organizational level, habits are called *norms* ("how we do things around here"). People quickly become socialized to the norms and styles of acting common to the organizations of which they are a part. Norms often provide subtle yet powerful mechanisms that redirect deviant behavior and keep people in line. Suppose one of the norms in an organization is to keep conflict from surfacing; keep it submerged. If a new employee began to act rashly and aggressively, stirring up conflict, they would soon receive substantial—subtle and not so subtle—feedback from the organization that their way of behaving is not appropriate or acceptable. Gradually over time, perhaps entirely unconsciously, their creative energies would begin to manifest in behavior consistent with the organizational norms.

The availability and flow of *information* is another powerful organizational structure. Here, the crucial questions are: "How do people obtain the information they need to get their jobs done?" "Do they have free access to all the information they need, or is some of it kept accessible only to certain powerful people in the organization?" Suppose that everyone recognizes

194

the importance of open, honest interaction among employees, but some of the information individuals need to do their jobs is restricted and held in the hands of a designated few. Such a structure will foster the notion that information is equal to power. As a result, people's creative energies will be limited by the information they have available, and there will be a tendency to breed information monopolies, no matter how committed people say they are to open dialogue.

Finally, the *physical processes* that occur in an organization are structures that enormously influence how people channel their energies. In a paper manufacturing company, the structure and flow of a physical process might be traced in the many steps it takes to transform trees in the forest into rolls of tissue on supermarket shelves. Another physical process is the flow of written reports in an administrative system. It is the structure of an R&D department that governs the path of a new engineering project from idea, to preliminary design, to collecting the right design team, to the creation of detailed engineering layouts; or of an advertising department from a new promotional idea, to consumer research, to designing ads, filming them, purchasing air time, and delivering copies of recorded videocassettes to television stations. The accomplishment of these processes in the appropriate sequence and the movement of physical goods from step to step almost invariably imposes physical limitations on how the human beings in an organization use and channel the creative energies they possess.

Creative energy will flow consistent with the pressures or constraints of the control structures; with what people are rewarded for or paid to do; with personal and organizational goals, beliefs, values, long-standing habits, and norms; with the availability of information; and finally, in accordance with physical laws and the physical processes of the organization.

The power and beauty of these personal and organizational structures is that, once constructed, they operate almost automatically and require very little conscious attention. Because of this, we as individuals are able to devote the major part of our time and attention to the functions of formulating vision and consciously evolving the structures and processes to foster its manifestation.

Structural Conflicts

A real difficulty stems from the fact that there are many elements in each of the classes of structure mentioned above. Each of these elements interacts with others within its own group and with those of other groups. Often they contradict each other or are otherwise in conflict. For example, I can have goals that are inconsistent with what I am rewarded to do, with certain habits I or my organization may have, even with other personal goals. In an organization, certain desired habits may be inconsistent with what is rewarded, or what is rewarded may be in conflict with important values. The possibilities are endless. The result is one elaborate, interrelated system of structural elements that largely governs the performance of individuals and the organization. As individuals, we each live with many demands and yearnings pulling us this way and that. Symbolically, it is as if we had thousands of rubber bands around our waist connected to different structures in our lives—sets of beliefs, values, habits, norms, physical processes, rewards, incentives—each of which creates tension that constrains or otherwise influences our behavior. In combination, some sets of rubber bands act to hold us in healthy balance. Some move us toward what we want, while others are contradictory, diffuse our energy, and pull us in different directions.

Likewise in an organization some of the structures that seem to be in conflict with others can actually be helping to maintain a healthy balance in support of the overall vision. For example, suppose there is a conflict between some goal we want right now and one of our basic values. Our inability to immediately reconcile the discrepancy may cause us to ask which of the two results is more important to us. Such a conflict keeps us on track by challenging us to reflect upon who we are and what we truly want to create.

Since some of these contradictory structures do, in fact, cause us to work at cross purposes and expend our creative energies getting nowhere, structural conflict in organizations is generally viewed as undesirable. And some of it obviously is. Just as frequently, however, having cross tension in organizations can be quite healthy.

The job of leadership in a metanoic organization is to keep the primary structures, such as goals and values, continually in the organizational focus, so that a conflict among subordinate structures is always viewed from the larger focus. Leaders will also want to augment present structures with additional ones that enhance the flow of creative energy in alignment with the organization's purpose. Finally, leaders should always be seeking to identify those structural conflicts that are, in fact, dysfunctional and should be dismantled.

Leader as Designer of Structure

The most neglected aspect of leadership is that of design. Imagine that your organization is like an ocean liner and that you are the leader of it. What analogous role would you occupy in relation to the ocean liner? The most common response is "captain." But the person who has the greatest actual influence on the ship's performance is not the captain. It is the naval architect who designed the ship. No captain can get great performance from a ship that, because of its design, tends to list in the water or can't turn. The way a ship—or an organization—is designed is vitally important.

Because structural design is a major influence of organizational performance, it is an exceedingly important leadership role. However, it has often remained unappreciated for one obvious reason: the consequence of a great design is the absence of problems. When a system is working without problems, its great design is more or less invisible; it usually goes unnoticed and unrewarded. In contrast, what does get noticed in organizations are *problems*, and what gets rewarded are the people who solve them. We tend to recognize, reward, and read management books about the white knights who ride in on their white stallions to save the day, rather than those leaders who design great structure.

197

For years, one of our major objectives as managers has been to engineer the optimum organization, that is, to obtain the highest performance while maintaining stability and predictability. Our hope was to design a set of structures in which one only needed to replace any departing worker with another person of moderately equal talent and the organization would experience no loss in performance. To my knowledge, there has been no evidence that such a mechanistic orientation has ever led to inspired performance. Inspired performance is a function of inspired people operating with vision and purpose in well-conceived organizational structures, ones that are designed primarily to foster the creation of a collective vision and to channel the creative energies of everyone toward producing the results to which they are all committed.

Leadership and Intuition

Often, leading a metanoic organization seems overwhelming in its complexity. And if you were to approach the task with solely rational capacities, it would be. Fortunately, we have been provided with the capacity for intuition, which we can use to help simplify the enormous complexity of life. Intuition is a tool used by all great leaders to formulate and validate their visions, establish empathy and rapport with their followers, and deal with the convoluted and systemic relationships among structural elements.

However, intuition alone is insufficient. Metanoic organizations cannot be led by fiat. So, no matter how accurate your intuitive insights are, they must be confirmable through rational analysis in order to be seen as plausible by others in the organization. Moreover, when you lack a rational confirmation of what you sense to be right, it is all too easy to be swayed away from your vision by another's rational argument, even when you know intuitively they are wrong.

Great organizational leaders, like great scientists, use intuition and rationality to complement each other. They guide their analyses with their intuition, and they verify their intuitive insights with rational analysis. In this way, at the deepest levels, leaders in a metanoic organization will apprehend the organization as a whole entity rather than as a machine-like aggregation of autonomous parts. They will know how people can operate independently yet interconnectedly to bring about results consistent with their dreams.

To create and lead a metanoic organization requires that you create and integrate your own versions of the ideas presented in this article. It also likely requires that you continue to build upon many of the activities you have been doing all along. It may require also that in the future you implement numerous leadership abilities we have yet to discover.

It would be nice if creating and leading a metanoic organization only required one to have a vision for the organization. In my experience, although formulating an organizational vision is paramount, the other two leadership abilities—enrolling and empowering others and designing functional structures—are just as essential.

The development of these skills and abilities is likely to be a lifelong task. But the commitment to a vision of your organization's greatness is something immediately available to you, should you choose it. It arises from that deepest part of you from which your leadership naturally and non-manipulatively emerges and will provide a powerful wellspring of energy to inspire all your actions. Connected to your own sense of destiny and purpose, and supported by its unfailing wisdom, you and the people around you will be able to achieve results that transcend the ordinary and manifest the highest in human aspiration.

CAROL SANFORD is a partner in Sanford and Ely Associates, based in Washington State. Her practice is founded upon the understanding of fundamental scientific premises as well as ancient and modern teachings. She has worked with clients in Europe, Asia, and North America.

She received her M.A. in Public Law and Industrial Economics and her master's in Business and Urban Studies. Her doctoral dissertation was "Designed Change in Large Complex Systems." Her published works include *The Culture of Continuous Improvement, Science into Technique: A Structure for Research and Development in Organizational Science,* and *The Scientific Basis of Developmental Organizations: Some Thoughts and Examples,* all by Spring Hill Publications.

Pamela Mang, V.P. Marketing of Advanced Design Technologies, based in Santa Fe, New Mexico, collaborated in writing this chapter and has coauthored a book with Ms. Sanford, which will be released in the fall of 1992.

13

A Self-Organizing Leadership View of Paradigms

Carol Sanford

On hearing news of a new companywide training program, a weary manager expressed his frustration over the waves of such programs he had seen come and go over the last few years. When someone disagreed, noting that this one seemed to have some real potential, he responded, "Just wait—after a few months of beat-to-fit and paint-to-match, it will look like everything else that's rolled through here." Unfortunately for the company, his prediction was accurate. And even more unfortunately for all of us, the same process is being played out almost daily in offices and plants around the country.

There is growing recognition in the business world that old assumptions and methods seem to work less and less often. An abundance of new ones are being offered, but how to choose? Quality circles? Self-Managed Teams? Power of Positive Thinking? Ropes Courses? Total Quality Management? Just in Time? At an alarming rate, and in every domain (not just business), landmarks are crashing down or just slowly dissolving into what seems at times to be an ever-thickening fog of conflicting theories, dictums, and predictions. From time to time a startling new idea comes along that seems to sweep the fog away and make the landscape clear once again. But, just as quickly, another new idea, and then another one, comes on its heels, and the fog drops like a wet blanket, thicker than ever.

Even when a path seems clear, implementation of the change looms as an even larger challenge. For business leaders struggling to introduce fundamental change in order to better equip their organizations to meet a rapidly changing environment, it can seem at times as if there is some invisible, inordinately powerful gravitational force that works against movement or, if movement does occur, slowly but inevitably draws things back toward their original conditions. Every once in a while, fundamental lasting change seems to occur in some corner of one's own or someone else's business. But then, most frustrating of all, when the apparent causes are duplicated elsewhere, the results too often are the same cycle of resistance and regression.

In fact, such a force does exist, and it is both invisible and inordinately powerful. That it is invisible does not, however, mean it cannot be seen, only that we must learn new ways of seeing. And as to its inordinate power, it is a little like the Wizard of Oz. Once seen, we realize that we ourselves are the source of its power. This chapter is about learning to see and to utilize this force in order to bring leadership to the self-creation of our organizations as "self-organizing leaders."

The Ties That Bind

The force we refer to is the paradigm (sometimes called "worldview") that we and fellow members of our society adhere to. Thomas Kuhn, who is generally credited with developing the paradigm concept in 1947, described the role of paradigms in the shaping of all scientific thought in his enormously influential book, *The Structure of Scientific Revolutions*, published in 1962.

Soon after his ideas were published, they were being applied to all of human society. In the process, the word

202

"paradigm" took on a life of its own and, unfortunately, not always one that did justice to the original depth and power of Kuhn's work. Our intent here is to recapture the potential of his paradigm concept so it can be applied as an instrument of a new and powerful form of leadership that we call self-organizing leadership.

Jeremy Rifkin once described paradigms as having a "hold over our perception of reality so overwhelming that we can't possibly imagine any other way of looking at the world." Scientist John Casti's metaphor gives us a glimpse of how this works. Casti compares our knowledge of the world to the *terra incognita* of ancient mapmakers and a paradigm to the map that evolves through a series of explorations and adjustments. At first fairly crude, its details are filled in with each new wave of returning explorers, creating some confusion in the initial stages, but ultimately creating a widely accepted picture of reality.

This analogy is helpful in understanding the construction as well as the function of a paradigm. One need only recall the experience of trying to reach a destination in a strange city. Without a map we have no way of knowing where to look, how to plan, and little or nothing by which to orient ourselves. In attempting to understand how a paradigm binds us to it with such an overwhelming "hold over our perception of reality," we must analyze how a map and a paradigm differ, rather than how they are similar. When we use a map, we know that it is no more than an instrument for guidance that may or may not be current. As we move about, we use our own perceptions and experiences to continuously assess its accuracy and make choices about how much to rely on it. In contrast, we treat our paradigm as the territory (reality) itself rather than someone's best estimate of it.

Most of us remain unaware of our paradigm and unable to separate ourselves from it. As a result, without our knowledge or our choice, it shapes what we are able to see and, therefore, what we are able to do. If a map fails to conform to what we encounter on our walk through the city, we assume it is outdated and either look for a new one or strike out on our own.

When we encounter events that do not fit our paradigm's picture of reality, however, our response is to ignore or rationalize away the conflicting evidence.

Of Maps, Paradigms, and Leadership

There are increasing indications that the chaos we are experiencing is the result of trying to navigate a 20th-century world using a 17th-century map and, most important, not being able to distinguish between the map and the world. The last sixty years have been rich with the discoveries of new geographer/explorers, but so firmly entrenched is our 17th-century picture of reality, that we exhibit remarkable inventiveness and determination in our drive to beat-to-fit and paint-to-match every new and "world-shaking" discovery. When we do so we have succumbed, once again, to the force of our own mind's attachment to the old map or paradigm, no matter how inconsistent it seems to be with our own experience in the new territory. And each time we do so, we have created a small act of murder—the murder of our own potential as creative beings.

So what's a leader to do? Returning to Casti's analogy, when the reports of discrepancies between the standard map and what had been actually observed reached a certain level, the Society of Explorers determined that it was time "to shift their allegiance to a new firm of mapmakers whose pictures of the territory seemed more in line with the reports of the returning adventurers." Unfortunately for today's business leader trying to steer her or his firm through newly bewildering territory, there is no Society of Explorers to collect data and determine the validity of the maps. Even if there were, new discoveries and new interpretations are now coming so rapidly that no central authorizing body could possibly keep up. We find ourselves confronting not only new and unknown challenges but also a plethora of maps and mapmakers, each proclaiming the truth of their map. More and more, each business leader must sort through the explorers' reports, comparing them with their personal experience and inner knowledge, to become, if not their own mapmaker, at least a more capable judge of maps.

This capability is key to self-organizing leadership—a new form of leadership needed to meet the challenges and opportunities of a transition time. The central role of these leaders will be to reach out beyond the confining boundaries of the existing maps through seeing and anticipating the new order as it unfolds and through creating visions that guide themselves and others to see and participate in the creation of their own destiny—as organizations and individuals. To be able to do so, they must first build the capability to see and to organize their own thinking as a means of seeing and making choices about the paradigm that will guide them and their organization. It is exactly for this purpose that Kuhn's structural definition of paradigms is so powerful.

A Structural View of Paradigms

Scientists have long known the power of understanding something in terms of its underlying structure. Kuhn's work moved us from a philosophical concept of a "world view" to the more utilitarian theory of "paradigm," which he defined as a "constellation of group commitments" shared by a particular (scientific) community. These key elements, adapted somewhat to apply here, are:

> • **Symbolic generalizations**. Deployed without question or dissent by group members, they often take on the appearance of laws of nature and serve as banners around which a community forms its goals. Frequently represented in formula or slogan form, they trigger in the mind a fixed set of relationships and consequences.

> • **A set of beliefs in particular models of reality**. These models supply us with "preferred or permissible analogies and metaphors"—a powerful means of communicating ideas, knowledge, and understanding, while at the same time stimulating and focusing the community's response to its environment. In particular, these analogies and metaphors define, and thereby limit us to, what is "real," what is possible, and what is impossible and shape our priorities accordingly.

205

• **A set of fundamental values.** We use these values to validate or discard theories that explain and predict how events relate and unfold. These values provide a touchstone for measuring whether something is on or off course.

• **A set of puzzle-solutions or shared exemplars.** It is these shared exemplars (in business: case studies, on-the-job training, etc.) that may have the greatest impact on reinforcing and communicating a particular paradigm. Through the sharing of these approaches, we crystallize within ourselves a "time-tested and group-licensed way of seeing." These are profoundly useful social instruments. However, when we divorce them from the belief-based models and value-based theories from which they derive their validity, they become instead powerful shackles that tie us to the past, even if we no longer believe in it.

Putting this constellation of elements into graphic form, we might depict their structure as follows:

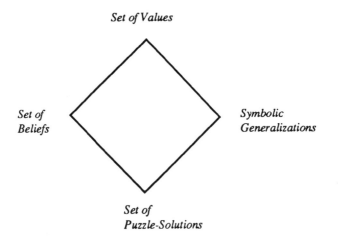

Set of Values

Set of Beliefs

Symbolic Generalizations

Set of Puzzle-Solutions

In this structured view of paradigms, our beliefs shape the motivation behind our actions, while the symbolic generalizations serve to shape the goals toward which our actions are aimed. Our values help us monitor and guide the direction of our actions while the puzzle-solutions shape the way we carry them out.

We can use Kuhn's structure as a "map reading" instrument that can help leaders organize our thinking to see how our current "map" or paradigm now shapes our daily business activities. This structure also provides a framework for understanding, assessing, and integrating the work of the new geographers and explorers into a new map to better guide business adventures.

Mechanical Paradigm

The current, and currently unraveling, Machine Age or Mechanical Paradigm has held sway in the Western world for over three hundred years. While it has evolved over this period, it has retained many fundamental premises that still dominate the infrastructure of thinking and organizing in modern business. One of the core beliefs that set it apart from its predecessors was the gift of Isaac Newton—that all of nature could be subjected to the laws of mathematics. In a world run by immutable, completely knowable, and observable laws, a mechanical model is a natural outcome. With machine as metaphor, the major preoccupation became the creation and sustenance of a stable environment conducive to the unbroken production of material worth. Error and degradation are our enemies; control of nature their remedy. As Locke wrote, ". . . land that is left wholly to nature . . . is called, as indeed it is, waste."

On the value point, René Descartes and Francis Bacon both contributed to the value for "objective" knowledge that marks this paradigm. From Descartes came the faith that we could master the world by unraveling its truths and the conviction that there is always a "right" answer to be found. In a world that values sharply defined good and bad, any theory (or person) that doesn't point to an orderly, predictable sequence of events toward desired goals is quickly discarded.

As to symbolic generalizations, "progress" and cause/effect became the banners behind which scientists, politicians

207

and business people have marched with full confidence that, if we are diligent, hard working, and hard-nosed, life will proceed in a straight line with each stage materially better than the last.

Bacon's gift to this worldview was the ideal puzzle-solution—the Scientific Method—a tidy and "purely objective" means of ascertaining the nature of the "real" world that relied on the belief that we could segment the messy world of nature into tidy little packets that could be measured, analyzed, and categorized. It worked so well in the physical world that its carryover to the world of living beings was almost a foregone conclusion. People became subject to, and could be understood in terms of, the same mechanical laws as machines. What couldn't be studied objectively was dismissed as irrelevant.

Using Kuhn's paradigm structure, we could depict the underlying structure of the Mechanical Paradigm as follows:

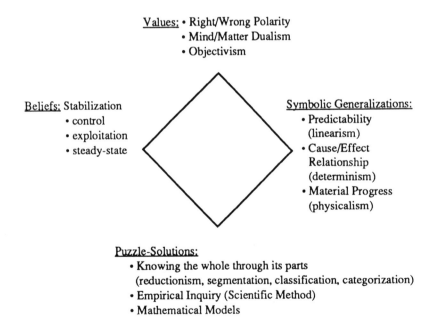

Values: • Right/Wrong Polarity
• Mind/Matter Dualism
• Objectivism

Beliefs: Stabilization
• control
• exploitation
• steady-state

Symbolic Generalizations:
• Predictability (linearism)
• Cause/Effect Relationship (determinism)
• Material Progress (physicalism)

Puzzle-Solutions:
• Knowing the whole through its parts (reductionism, segmentation, classification, categorization)
• Empirical Inquiry (Scientific Method)
• Mathematical Models

The Emerging Paradigm

While there is growing consensus that the current turbulence marks the emergence of a new paradigm, there is less agreement on the precise makeup of that paradigm, and therefore on what to call it. To avoid the controversy of labeling something that is still in process, we call it here simply the Emerging Paradigm. There is, however, growing agreement on its general nature and some of its key landmarks.

Instead of the cool clockwork of an hermetically sealed universe run according to immutable laws and driven by the need for stabilization, we see emerging a view of a constantly changing and dynamic world of interconnected systems in which chaos is a nurturing environment for the spontaneous regeneration of increasingly higher orders of creation.

Using Kuhn's map-reading instrument, we could depict the current understanding of the Emerging Paradigm's underlying structure as follows:

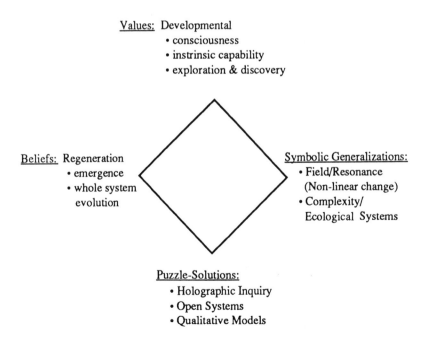

Values: Developmental
- consciousness
- instrinsic capability
- exploration & discovery

Beliefs: Regeneration
- emergence
- whole system
  evolution

Symbolic Generalizations:
- Field/Resonance
  (Non-linear change)
- Complexity/
  Ecological Systems

Puzzle-Solutions:
- Holographic Inquiry
- Open Systems
- Qualitative Models

Many of the ideas of the Emerging Paradigm are, in fact, quite ancient ones that are being given new depth and scientific underpinnings by a growing body of scientific and philosophical "explorer/geographers" who are nourishing its emergence. These include, but are by no means restricted to, such people as Ludwig von Bertalanffy, Ilya Prigogine, Erich Jantsch, David Bohm, Gregory Bateson, Rupert Sheldrake, and Karl Pribram.

Symbolic Generalizations

Because business is fundamentally concerned with change—in particular, how to create and manage it—the emerging concepts in this area are in many ways the most profoundly unsettling, with enormous implications for how we structure and conduct our businesses.

Most of our goals and practices around creating and managing change are still shaped by two related concepts about the nature of change that developed in the earliest stages of the Mechanical Paradigm and are now deeply embedded in our culture. Physicalism/determinism hold that all change is the result of the direct application of energy to matter, and that there is a directly traceable cause for every effect, and vise versa; the related concept of linearism holds that once launched (by the hand of man), change marches forward in a straight line. Implied in this is the expectation that we can indeed control change, but only if we are directly involved in it. In addition, non-directed change—change not visibly resulting from our effort—is seen only as an aberration, a variance from the plan. In fact, it is abundantly clear to anyone in business for more than a few years that control of change is more illusion and desire than reality, and just about the only predictable thing about change is that we can never predict all of its "side" or nonlinear effects. Yet managers continue to feel trapped by, on the one hand, the business's need to change more and more rapidly over greater and greater spans, and, on the other hand, the expectation that they must be "in control" of and directly involved in that change in order to manage it.

Moving toward a new paradigm, the work of biochemist Rupert Sheldrake and other researchers presents us with a

210

concept of change as transmittable through an invisible nonmaterial field of living energy. Sheldrake, who describes the process as "reality is habit forming," postulates that we create a kind of memory, a set of assumptions and patterns in our social fields, which conditions the way everyone in that field sees things. When a shift in these patterns reaches a critical threshold, it becomes pervasive beyond any space and time connection. In effect, it creates a new field to which people resonate, causing new habits for the social group. Learning becomes easier for each succeeding group because the field in which they exist is forming a new pattern and reconditioning the whole, a phenomenon we have seen now in several businesses. Once the threshold has passed, the new learning does not even need to be taught—it is just known by all within that field.

Puzzle-Solutions

One of the most far-reaching advances of the Mechanical Paradigm was the scientific method—the puzzle-solving process that seemed to bring order to messy, disorderly nature through the process of segmentation, and categorization or classification. Unfortunately, as the machine metaphor extended to people as well as the universe, and "nonmeasurable" dimensions such as consciousness, spirit, and thinking were discounted as irrelevant, the scientific method was distorted into a source for categorizing and segmenting people by type and organizing them based on hierarchical and categorical classes. As a result, we began to lose the ability to see the wholeness of each individual and their uniqueness in a business enterprise setting. We developed a wide array of fine-tuned and costly instruments for categorizing, classifying, and segmenting the performance of people. We take almost any process that could help us understand the totality of ourselves individually and collectively and convert it to a segmenting tool. As a result we are losing, or have lost, the valuing of diversity needed to gain wholeness and to support the heterostatic processes of regeneration required to survive in our rapidly changing environment.

What are some of the hallmarks of an organization trapped in the segmentation model? People identify, and relate to, themselves and others as "types" on a packaged, preset behavioral classification model. Racism, sexism, and classism are often significant problems. Most sadly, people's ability to contribute is restricted not by their capability but by their job definition.

Stanford University brain researcher Karl Pribram and physicist David Bohm have articulated a theoretical base for developing and engaging consciousness based on a holographic metaphor in which the part is in the whole and the whole is in each part. What does this mean in a practical sense? As an example, instead of seeking to exclude "problem" people, we would recognize that they are only a reflection of the health of the whole system and can even help us identify where the system is not working. It also means that we can be connected to the whole by selecting a holistic slice of the organization that is reflective of the whole (e.g. all functions, levels, perspectives) as the decision-making team for an entity. These replace the hierarchical decision processes wherein a decision, even when made at the "appropriate level," misses the whole and therefore misses critical considerations and learning processes.

The holographic model also requires us to look at each individual as unique, continuously developing and having the possibility of making an increasing value-adding contribution. Our challenge is to collaborate with people as a leader to discover, develop, and match that uniqueness to the contributions that are needed by the business.

Holographic thinking changes our perceptions about who are leaders. As Bob Porter, Du Pont's Memphis plant manager reflected, "I have to catch myself, stop myself from thinking that all the communication and leadership is my job. Watching an operator or a mechanic stand in front of his peers and superiors (including me), providing leadership to major change efforts and projects is really inspirational to me. What I am living is a fundamental change in the way I always thought about being a leader, but I feel really alive." In a similar vein, Rod Lawrence, operations manager of James River Paper, recently stated, "For the last few years, multilevel development has been our standard. I didn't know how rich and creative this was until I was recently put in a more traditional process. I really feel poorer when I'm not learning with operators on a regular basis."

Values

The great seductiveness of the universe-as-machine metaphor and the scientific method was their promise that, as an impartial and separate observer, one could finally understand the universe completely and finally know the right answers to age-old questions. Unfortunately, we have become a culture dominated by bipolar thinking, driven by the search for the "right" answer and certain that if we do not "know" the answer, we are doomed to failure. Furthermore, our value for separation of mind and matter often leads us to mistake facts for truth in that search.

Almost every facet of our educational system is based on value for having the right answers, the facts—our knowledge of the answer is our measure of our progress, first in school, then in business. When we don't have the answers, we hire consultants and experts to give them to us. At best, this polarity gives us an incomplete understanding; at worst it gives us dogma, tyranny, and war in our political and social contexts.

Gregory Bateson's work on learning how to learn postulates that it is possible to emerge into new thinking only when we can adopt a non-dualistic view of the world, one where mind and matter are not separated as Descartes had advocated. He felt that because of this dichotomy, we endanger accuracy and learning by the demand for objectivity (looking for only what we can see and count by using our senses in the material world). By this process we make life and interactions "thing-like" and therefore lose the spirit and higher values that we so wish for in our lives and organizations. As alternates, he offers value-based theories for building new learning processes that allow us to see the world in a new way, to see the relationships between multiple parts in a complex living system.

To be able to move our organization beyond duality, we need a model of development that includes consciousness and capability and thrives on diversity and wholeness. Charles Krone has differentiated development from growth and learning as a way of understanding how being guided by development in the Emerging Paradigm differs from the growth-dominated model of the Mechanical Paradigm. Growth, which has a fixed end point and requires nutrients from the environment, is a precondition to development but is not sufficient in the emergent paradigm. Development is the process of increasing our scope and power to do *and* to be. It is more focused on bringing potential, that which has not yet been manifested, into actuality. Unlike growth, its source of nourishment is from within. We can only develop by doing something new or by causing movement in a new direction, taking on something we do not readily know how to do. This places a demand on us to find more of ourselves, to learn more about ourselves, and to develop more in ourselves.

Conclusion

The next generation of business vision will come from those able to disrupt their own, and others', currently dominant patterns of thinking. One source for this "self-disruption" is the rapidly advancing wave of discoveries being made by emerging paradigm explorers. The holographic and holistic nature of their work has made possible a rapid extension of their fundamental premises to all domains of business—not just the technology—at a rate unmatched in human history. A second source for new vision is the creativity that emerges as leaders develop the flexibility and confidence to become explorers themselves and lead explorations into the unknown.

Finding ways to tap into these emerging discoveries, and uncover one's own capability to see new and previously unperceivable and unconceivable approaches, is both the opportunity and the challenge for those who would become self-organizing leaders—those leaders who will guide the self-creation of their organizations' and of their own destinies.

DR. JOHN W. THOMPSON is founder, president, and chief executive officer of Human Factors, Inc., a California international management consulting company that works primarily with the key executives and senior management of Fortune 500 companies. He is also the founder and chairman of the board of Acumen International, Inc., an educational software company focused on the application of expert-based computer technology to management and leadership assessment and development.

Dr. Thompson has been in the educational field for the last two decades and has delivered educational programs to well over one hundred thousand professionals. Over the last decade, he has developed a powerful technology for organizational change based on sound principles derived from the natural sciences. He has published numerous articles as well as the book *The Human Factor: An Inquiry into Communication and Consciousness.*

14

Corporate Leadership in the 21st Century

John W. Thompson

The crisis is in our consciousness, not in the world.
—J. K. Krishnamurti

Introduction

In an environment where changes in world conditions are occurring so rapidly that the very ground gives way like quicksand and business challenges continually emerge that our contemporary ways of thinking and behaving are inadequate to solve, our corporate executives are frantically seeking new models for success. To do this, corporate leaders must somehow see out beyond the horizon of emerging events. As we approach the 21st century, visionary leadership is no longer just desirable; it is rapidly becoming the cornerstone of corporate survival.

In this emerging crisis, it will not be enough to issue general calls for visionary leadership. Business executives need more than vague, abstract notions of leadership. They need to know exactly what human qualities are called for and how to elicit those traits in themselves and others.

It is my position that the leadership qualities that will now be required of corporate executives are *not* skills that can be learned. Our research reveals that these qualities are latent capacities that rest unused, and often unsuspected, in the recesses of the human mind and spirit. My premise is that leadership is not exceptional, but the natural expression of the fully functional personality. As Warren Bennis put it, "The process of becoming a leader is much the same as becoming an integrated human being." The burning question is why these qualities are not expressed more commonly in corporate executives.

I believe it will become widely understood that we are mentally and emotionally shackled in our expression of leadership. These shackles, initially forged in the family crucible, are later hardened in our school system and then reinforced in the corporate world.

In this chapter, I will present the Visionary Leadership Inventory, a new software-based psychometric instrument, which provides a practical, specific, and highly articulated picture of the central qualities required for corporate leadership in the 21st century. I will also describe a system of leadership development that, in the past decade, has helped thousands of corporate clients to break through unconscious childhood conditioning and bring forward and apply their latent leadership capabilities in a way that dramatically improves corporate performance and individual well being.

Treacherous Waters

Trying to grasp the depth of the predicament our corporate leaders currently face requires us to examine the phenomena of change more closely. When asked what has been the greatest failure of mankind to date, most observers usually point to our inability to coexist peacefully, the nuclear threat, the ecological disaster (including the destruction of the rain forest, pollution, depletion of the ozone layer, and global warming), hunger in the Third World, etc. Rather than any of these, I believe that our greatest failure to date has been mankind's failure to take into account the mathematical exponential function, a basic concept of physical science.

Our experience of change is primarily linear rather than exponential. We expect the *rate* of change to remain constant over repeated, equally spaced intervals rather than increasing with each measurement. When we hear of an earthquake registering a seven on the seismic scale, we think of it as "somewhat" more powerful than an earthquake registering a six, when in fact it is ten times more powerful while an eight is one hundred times stronger.

While we don't notice it, the fact is that changes of all kinds on our planet tend to follow a curve that more closely approximates the e-function than a linear one. What does this mean? Consider the change in information in modern times. Up until the time of Newton in the 17th century, one person could still know almost all there was to be known in the entire world! That was less than four hundred years ago. Today, that possibility is so far out of reach it is almost inconceivable that it was once possible. Now, in 1991 we are in a rate of change in information so great it is difficult for the human mind to grasp. This phenomenon is illustrated in the following diagram.

e - FUNCTION AND RATES OF CHANGE

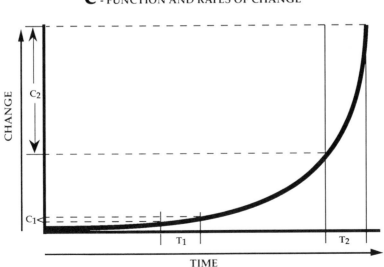

Perceptual Distortion

The problem of exponential change is insidious in that when the rate of change becomes fast enough, our perceptual mechanisms have difficulty registering and assimilating what is happening. Our minds are calibrated to look for linear change. The condition may be out of control before we even notice that any significant change has taken place. In other words, exponential change sort of sneaks up on us and then overwhelms us before we can respond.

An example of this was reported in *Scientific American* a few years ago after scientists began to use computers to look for and record changes in the ozone level in our atmosphere. The satellite system measuring ozone levels above the south pole was programmed to ignore as obviously spurious any recorded changes above certain levels. According to their expectations at that time, ozone levels were unlikely to vary above certain rates, so any data indicating a more rapid decrease could be rejected as erroneous. Thus the explosive growth of the now-famous "ozone hole" above Antarctica went undetected for several years, until raw data from the satellite was re-analyzed by scientists who had developed a premise that the rate of deterioration of the ozone level had actually reached previously unimaginable proportions.

The central point is that conventional ways of thinking, analyzing data, problem solving, decision making, and responding to changing world conditions, acceptable at the rates of change in world conditions we faced from 1900 (time of the birth of our modern corporations) through the 1970s, are fundamentally obsolete and inadequate in the 1990s. The '80s marked a segue into a grim new reality for the American economic community: a world moving into blinding rates of change while traditional ways of responding failed.

Peter Vaill, describing the condition we have entered as "permanent white water" says that now

> *executives cannot count on the presence of markets; the availability of technologies; the likely actions of competi-*

tors, foreign and domestic, and of legislators and regula-
tory bodies; or the reactions of employees, of their families
and, indeed of their own bodies and minds to the kind of
actions they are contemplating. . . .

In these treacherous waters, faced with these seemingly impossible conditions, where do corporate leaders turn to succeed, indeed to survive? In 1989, the Columbia University School of Business and Korn/Ferry International published a report on "Reinventing the CEO" based upon questionnaires completed by more than fifteen hundred CEOs and other senior executives, representing corporations that *collectively produce 10 percent of the Gross World Product.* The study covered the Pacific Rim, South America, Europe, and the United States. According to this detailed and thoughtful report, executives overwhelmingly "stressed the vital importance of visionary leadership." In their view, this kind of leadership includes anticipating the corporation's future and its place in global business, setting ambitious corporate goals, and inspiring managers to achieve them.

Since products and even entire markets are becoming "as transient as cherry blossoms," the report says, the CEO will increasingly be required to "formulate a strategy for surmounting threats that have not yet materialized." Making the military metaphor explicit, the authors declare that the new leader will "identify enemies before they themselves realize they are adversaries, anticipate weapons before they have been invented, and attack before anyone else realizes there is a battle to fight."

This then is the unprecedented challenge corporate leaders face as we look toward the 21st century, but as the authors of this report note with concern, "There is powerful evidence that the size and diversity of the American marketplace, and a history of economic pre-eminence are blinding American CEOs to the demand for these skills." Throughout the last thirty years, corporate leaders in the United States have largely thought and acted as though our past economic success would guarantee future success. And so we ignored the hurricane of change bearing down on us.

221

Research, such as the Korn/Ferry report, suggests that leadership in the new order will involve qualities beyond visionary foresight. In addition, success will rest on abilities to "imbue the corporation with a sense of purpose and direction" to "inspire managers to implement the optimistic visions of corporations," to "imbue the organization with energy and inspire employees to realize their potential." Other qualities referred to repeatedly include integrity, creativity, enthusiasm, open-mindedness, intuition, risk-taking, collaboration, and diplomacy.

These qualities, for the most part, are reported in the psychological literature as the natural expression of the healthy, well-integrated personality. If this is so, then one must conclude that their failure to appear more abundantly in our corporate executives and managers reflects not some exotic skill set to be learned but, rather, like the hidden ozone hole referred to earlier, a dysfunctional cultural condition so pervasive and widespread as to render the problem, and its root causes, invisible to other than a highly trained eye.

Roots of the Problem

In science, emerging paradigms, or theories, compete in their attempts to answer as yet unanswered questions. Charles Darwin's theory of evolution, proposed in his *Origin of the Species,* is an example of such a new paradigm contributing to a breakthrough in our understanding of the world we live in. Albert Einstein's general theory of relativity is another. Today we stand on the verge of such a breakthrough in understanding in the field of psychology.

Over the past thirty years a consensus has arisen among the various branches of psychology concerned with personality formation and treatment of psychological dysfunctions that the absence of the ability to express oneself in healthy, natural ways as described earlier may be almost entirely attributed to how we are reared as children and later educated.

Consider this: there is less training required today to conceive, bear, and rear a child than to obtain a driver's license!

222

Our only guide for raising and teaching our children is our personal experience of being raised at the hands of our parents. In this way our methods of child rearing have been simply passed on generation to generation, largely without question or challenge until very recently.

The rules that primarily govern parenting and personality formation have largely not changed for the last 150 years. These rules grew out of a scientific, philosophical, and theological view of human nature that arose from Isaac Newton's view of the world. Newton conceived the world much like the machines emerging from the Industrial Revolution. Thinking and reasoning were king. Emotions and desire could contaminate and were suspicious. Emotions must be controlled by reason. John Bradshaw describes the traditional role of the parent, arising from this worldview, in these stark terms:

> *Mothers and fathers carried God's authority. Their task was to teach their children the laws of God and nature and to be sure they obeyed these laws. Emotions and willfulness had to be repressed. Children were born with an unruly animal nature. Their souls, although made in God's image, had been stained by original sin. Therefore, children needed discipline. Great energy had to be spent in breaking their unruly passions and their unbridled spirit. Spare the rod and you spoil the child. . . . Good children are defined as meek, considerate, unselfish and perfectly law-abiding. Such rules leave no place for vitality, spontaneity, inner freedom, inner independence and critical judgement.*

For the most part, then, what has passed for child rearing in the Western world is what is recognized today, in psychology, as a form of behavioral conditioning that focuses on punishment and rewards.

In the family system, this kind of approach revolves around the parents' role as "God," requiring children to disorient from their own values, intuition, thoughts, and feelings and orient themselves around the parents' view of what is right and wrong. A child's failure or refusal to mold to the parents demands and expectations results in repeated verbal, emotional, or physical punishment (raised voices, anger, a slap, shaking, or a spanking). Successfully shaping oneself to the parents' beliefs and intentions results in repeated verbal, emotional, and physical rewards (praise, love, hugs, and kisses). In this way, just like programming a computer, the child's mind becomes programmed with parental notions of what is right and proper.

As a result the child gradually becomes less and less attuned to his or her own inner wisdom, what Abraham Maslow termed "the wisdom of the organism," and more and more attuned to the approval and acceptance of others. To be accepted by others, to be loved, the child is driven to override a vital internal process of understanding what she or he actually values and desires.

It is worthy of note that these traditional methods of disciplining children are now characterized, in clinical psychology, as verbal, emotional, and physical abuse. It is further important to note that the bulk of our corporate leaders today were born between 1930 and 1950, a period of time when such approaches to parenting were almost universally practiced.

What is lost in this parenting process is what Bradshaw termed the "natural child" or "authentic child," which is the natural expression of our own inner values and desires. This natural child, our true self, is the source of intuition, creativity, curiosity, enthusiasm, and *all the other qualities that have come to be recognized as visionary leadership.* Visionary leadership, then, may be most clearly understood to be the free and authentic expression of our true inner spirit.

It was not only the family that was shaped by the Newtonian model but our educational system and modern corporation as well. Our educational system is structured largely around *what* to think rather than *how* to think. As Abraham Maslow stated it,

> *Educators focus on implanting the greatest possible amount of information in the greatest number of children, with a minimum of time, expense and effort. . . . Children in the usual classroom learn very quickly that creativity is punished, while repeating a memorized response is rewarded,*

and concentrate on what the teacher wants them to say, rather than understanding the problem. Since classroom learning focuses on behavior rather than on thought, the child learns exactly how to behave while keeping his thoughts his own.

Well into the '60s, physical punishment was commonly practiced on "unruly" students in our school system. For example, as a child I was hit on the hand with the edge of a heavy ruler for speaking during quiet periods and for serious infractions was "spanked" with a three foot board (drilled with holes for greater impact). Again, reflect on the fact that the bulk of our corporate leaders today were educated in this system.

Now consider the corporation, an institution traditionally organized around authority and control. Performance is managed primarily by punishment and reward. McGregor, in his classic book, *The Human Side of Enterprise*, recognized this abusive system as early as the '50s when he referred to the "carrot and stick" condition of organizations and stated that many organizational practices seem based on the belief that people dislike work and "must be coerced, controlled, directed, threatened" to produce. It is now widely recognized in psychology that in such a system, people unconsciously fall into familial patterns of thinking, behaving, and relating to one another. Authority figures (managers) become parents and subordinates become children, functioning largely out of the frozen false self that precludes the possibility of expression of spirit or the act of leadership. As Harry Levinson put it, "An organization is composed of persons in authority and 'siblings' who relate to those authorities." In these conditions, corporations begin to resemble dysfunctional families (as widely recognized in clinical psychology).

"A leader proficient in consciousness," says management consultant Robert Rabbin, "knows that the true source of qualities coveted by managers—commitment, vitality, creativity, responsibility—is within the inner heart of people, and the inner heart of people opens through the cultivation of spirit. These qualities cannot be fabricated by a manipulation of behavior through reward and punishment."

225

Collectively, conditions within these three institutions—the family, the educational system, and the corporation—represent an unconscious cultural conspiracy, held in silence, that deadens the human spirit and precludes the possibility of leadership.

If as Bennis suggests, and I have argued here, that leadership is the natural expression of the fully integrated person, then leadership development becomes the process of breaking up the patterned responses of the false self and learning to trust and express ourselves consistent with our true inner nature.

For leadership to succeed, for us to face the 21st century squarely, we must exhibit courage, the first characteristic of leadership as proclaimed by the Native American culture well before the advent of our modern corporations. To free ourselves from this great conspiracy, to break the shackles that restrain us, we must face the demons of our childhood wounds and risk the expression of our true inner nature in the workplace.

Solutions and Challenges

For the past thirty years, bodies of knowledge, largely held apart by Newtonian thinking in science and education, have begun to flow together and cross-fertilization has occurred. From this great confluence of the natural sciences, psychology and sociology, general semantics, systems theory, and the wisdom traditions, a portrait of authentic or conscious self-expression—the essence of visionary leadership—has been etched.

This portrait has been captured in a new, statistically sound, software-based psychometric instrument— the Visionary Leadership Inventory (VLI). This instrument, developed by researchers at Human Factors, Inc., measures eight core dimensions crucial to true leadership effectiveness. In developing the instrument, we began with this simple premise: leadership springs not from learnable techniques, a "style" that can be assumed, or some exotic skill set that can be taught, but rather from who people naturally are as human beings. Instead of trying to isolate a set of behaviors or skills, we examined states of mind, values, and orientation to life.

226

The Visionary Leadership Inventory covers eight dimensions:

Learning orientation: A passion for seeking new knowledge to improve self and others.

Self-Knowledge: A strong sense of self; comfort with one's own strengths and weaknesses.

Values Foundation: A firm anchoring in humanistic values; strong personal integrity.

Vision: An ability to see beyond "what is" to "what could be"; a strong sense of purpose.

Values Bridging: A commitment to set a foundation of humanistic values in the organization.

Vision Bridging: A commitment to unite the organization under a shared vision of the future.

Empowerment: A belief in people and their abilities; a commitment to draw out the best in others.

Organizational Sensitivity: An understanding of human behavior and how to influence others; diplomacy.

A New Operating System

In our work with corporate leaders, the VLI and other proprietary psychometric instruments provide a prelude to intensive individual and group work. This work helps participants discover and acknowledge their dysfunctional ways of thinking and behaving as leaders. They experience more effective alternatives and begin to develop a consciousness that will sustain new and more productive ways of thinking and functioning in the workplace.

It is our belief that you cannot "teach" or "bestow" leadership qualities on someone, any more than you can give them freedom. What you can do is create situations in which people recognize and express their own abilities and in which they are free to act. In short, you can elicit these qualities only by creating a world in which they are relevant.

As leaders discard old, unproductive patterns of thought and behavior and regain access to their inner wisdom, they become more integrated and whole. This expanded awareness brings with it an increased ability to cut through what the English poet William Blake called our "mind-forged manacles," thus liberating the human spirit and the ability to fully express oneself. How is this achieved?

Consider this analogy from science and technology, in this case from the world of computers. This new expression of leadership represents a change not at the level of data (thoughts), not even at the level of an applications program, such as Lotus 1.2.3, within which data are being processed (the thought process), but at the operating system level, the basic program that allows the various utilities to function, such as UNIX or MS DOS (the contextual framework of thinking). If our minds may be thought of as a bio-computer, then the computer's operating system can be likened to our basic programs for functioning in the world, developed in childhood and reinforced in the school system.

Although computer programmers are familiar with operating systems, most of us seldom, if ever, go behind the applications program. In a similar way, we are largely unconscious of the operating program built up by our conditioning in childhood. Conditioning does not prohibit us from functioning but makes it difficult for us to change or even to be aware, on a conscious level, of what we are doing. It is easily possible to demonstrate, that, contrary to popular belief, the vast majority of our day-to- day thoughts and behaviors are not creative or spontaneous but constrained, programmed, and completely predictable.

In our leadership development programs, we lead clients through the experience of examining their own operating systems and then modifying these systems, expanding them in such a way as to enhance one's very " condition of mind." The level of change described here is at the level of deep reorganization of cognition—equivalent to moving from the limitations of a computer operating system such as MS DOS to a more powerful system like OS-2. Changes at this level liberate tremendous amounts of energy, allowing individuals to consciously choose their actions rather than being limited (or even run) by unconscious and automatic thought processes.

Once clients reach a new level of understanding about how they operate, new qualities begin to emerge; qualities that are innate but have been lost or suppressed by early conditioning. These deep qualities virtually always match up with those described in our portrait of visionary leadership. This is how we can attest that leadership is the natural expression of a fully integrated person.

The end result of such work is that executives become much more self-observant and are more able to determine what patterns of thinking and behavior are dysfunctional expressions arising from the false self and to discard them in favor of new, more authentic expressions of their inner desires and intentions—the essential expression of leadership.

As participants experiment with attitudes and behavior arising from authentic, genuine self-expression, conditions begin to emerge they previously only dreamed of, intuitively knew existed, but never dared expect in the corporate setting—courage, truthfulness, vulnerability, a sense of unification and belonging, love, trust, intimacy, support and respect, openness, self-responsibility, and, finally, playfulness and wonder.

To summarize, at its foundation, true leadership is the authentic outward expression of the inner character of an individual. True leaders listen to a deep inner wisdom, speak from the heart, and act with integrity and courage. They inspire others toward extraordinary achievement by the strength of their vision, the clarity of their purpose, and their unswerving commitment to personal integrity. It is not what visionary leaders do that makes them extraordinary; it is who they are as human beings.

As corporate CEOs and other executives face the 21st century, the challenge is clearly drawn. The qualities required to meet this hurricane of change bearing down on us have been clearly articulated by thoughtful chief executives around the world. The understanding of what has restrained us is at hand and the technology for change is available. The outcome is in our hands; the choice is ours. Corporate success in the 21st century will stand on courage—the courage to face ourselves and the courage to address our future with wisdom and spirit.

KENNETH H. BLANCHARD, Ph.D., coauthor of *The One Minute Manager* with Spencer Johnson, M.D., received his B.A. and Ph.D. from Cornell University. His text *Management of Organizational Behavior: Utilizing Human Resources,* coauthored with Paul Hersey, is considered standard reading on the subject of management.

He is founder of a California-based management consulting firm, Blanchard Training and Development, Inc. He maintains a faculty position in leadership at the University of Massachusetts, Amherst, as well as being on the board of trustees of Cornell University.

15

Ethics in American Business

Kenneth H. Blanchard

All across our country, there is evidence of a deterioration of ethics. Nowhere is this decline greater than in the world of business. Honest, caring, rational individuals seemingly have come to check their values at the door when they enter the office. The attitude in many businesses appears to be profit at any cost, especially if a company's gains can be at the expense of a competitor—and, sometimes, even if it is at the expense of its customers.

In a competitive business environment where anything goes, ethical considerations have come to be the first to go. Somehow, tough yet simple questions such as "Is this fair?" never get addressed because they are never brought up. Management may check for accuracy in accounting and, increasingly, look to see that quality is present in its products and services, but for the most part there is no systematic review of ethical considerations where review is needed most: in individual management and the corporate decision-making processes.

Simply bringing up an ethical consideration requires courage in most businesses, since the topic too often is assumed to pose problems rather than opportunities for management. When ethical considerations of proposed actions are weighed, there tends to be a hesitancy and awkwardness in the discussion, perhaps in part because such discussions are seldom held but also due to the unfounded belief that being ethical might not be best for business.

Is It Worth the Effort to Be Ethical?

Unfortunately, management in many businesses excludes ethical considerations because it has the notion there will be no financial benefit to the organization as a result of acting ethically. The evidence on the topic, however, point to the conclusion that being ethical does, in fact, make good business sense—financially and otherwise.

Long-term success

Studies indicate that successful companies over the long term tend to be ethical companies. For example, the Ethics Resource Center in Washington examined twenty one companies with a written code of principles stating that serving the public was central to their being. The center found that if you had invested $30,000 in a composite of the Dow Jones thirty years ago, it would be worth $134,000 today. If you had invested the same $30,000 in those companies in the survey, your $30,000 would be worth $1,021,861 today—almost nine times as much! In another study, Mark Pastin, director of the Center for Ethics at Arizona State University, found that a list of U.S. corporations that have paid dividends for one hundred years or more tends to coincided with those companies that make ethics a high priority.

Granted, this evidence *correlates* ethical practices with long-term business success and does not *prove* that being ethical will guarantee success. Such a guarantee cannot be made. Yet astute business managers know that business success and ethical practices go hand in hand. They have a broader focus on the purpose of business that supersedes daily activities of the business. They know that ultimately *there is no right way to do a wrong thing.*

We believe that good business focuses on developing and maintaining long-term relationships. A business person who makes a quick financial gain by taking advantage of customers, suppliers, or employees may show a slightly higher profit this quarter, but the trust that was lost in the process may never be restored to the business relationship. More times than not, the disgruntled customer will switch to a competitor as soon as it is convenient to do so. The day will come when a supplier that was taken advantage of will be able to gain the upper hand. And employees who feel they are treated unfairly by their employer will "even the score" in a dozen different ways: stealing supplies or inventory, padding expense accounts, making personal long-distance phone calls while at work, calling in sick on days they are well, and so on.

In fact, one measure of how ethical a company is can be found in how it handles its business relationships, including those with vendors, suppliers, and employees. Management at M&M Mars, the candy maker, realizes the importance of maintaining balance in long-term relationships. When an M&M Mars purchasing agent was able to get a greatly depressed discount on cacao beans, he proudly reported the news to the home office. Much to his chagrin, the home office wired back that he should renegotiate the order with more reasonable prices. The official explanation was that the company wasn't in business to take advantage of its suppliers when they were having a hard time. One never knows when the tables will be turned, and in a future year the company might be at the mercy of the supplier for vital resources.

Short-term benefits

Significant short-term benefits of being ethical exist as well, even though these benefits are often less tangible. For example, customers are increasingly sensitive to the perceived ethics of businesses they deal with. They stop doing business with some companies that they deem to be unethical and continue to work with, and refer others to, ethical enterprises.

Other benefits of being ethical are more psychological in nature. At the individual level, being ethical has a positive effect on self-esteem; at the organizational level, being ethical helps to build and maintain company pride.

Kenneth T. Derr, vice chairman of Chevron Corporation, says: "There's no doubt in my mind that being ethical pays, because I know in our company people who sleep well at night work better during the day." More than ever, organizational pride translates to the overall reputation of the company and, hence, the public's perception of how ethical a company is. And public perceptions can have a direct impact on a company's bottom line. For example, it is estimated that the long-standing boycott of Nestlé over its ethically questionable promotion of the company's infant formula in Third World countries cost that company over $40 million in lost revenues. And Union Carbide's stock took a nosedive because of their management's handling of the Bhopal, India, disaster.

All in all, when the evidence is examined, it is fair to conclude that the question "Does it pay to be ethical?" should more rightfully be "Does it pay *not* to be ethical?" From the unfolding insider-trading scandals on Wall Street led by Ivan Boesky and Dennis Levine to public officials caught in lies made without forethought, I contend that being ethical is the only way to prosper and survive in the long term.

How Can a Business Be More Ethical?

To be ethical, a company must make ethics a more tangible and discussable issue that is implemented on a daily basis. To facilitate this need, I have come to define an ethical situation as one that is governed by an agreed-upon code of behavior of a group to which you belong. This code of behavior can range from an employer's code of conduct to that of a social or a religious group. Almost always, the group's code is written down.

Develop a code of ethics

If a manager or employe is contemplating an action in conflict with the group's code of conduct, an ethical decision exists. If there are no generally agreed-upon guidelines in the situation, the choice of action becomes a moral choice, to be decided solely upon the values of those individuals involved. For this reason, I highly recommend that all organizations develop a code of ethics. Otherwise, some choices that employees might face will be handled differently (and, quite possibly, inconsistently) since individual values can vary widely from employee to employee.

A positive, well-documented example of an effective code is found at Johnson & Johnson. It begins:

> We believe that our first responsibility is to the doctors, nurses, and patients, to mothers and all others who use our products and services. In meeting their needs, everything we do must be of high quality.

Having this code in place helped management at McNeil Consumer Products Company, a wholly owned subsidiary of Johnson & Johnson, handle the Tylenol crisis a few years ago. The company's management had several options besides a total recall of thirty one million bottles of Tylenol at a cost of about $100 million. But, because management had a clear, written ethical credo to guide it, the decision to act in the best interests of the consumer was never in doubt. Within a matter of months the company was able to regain a majority share of the painkiller market with a new product. A strong customer bond remained unbroken through a time of duress, and the company's reputation for integrity and concern for the public good was greatly enhanced.

A clear policy or code needs to be communicated and enforced within a company. For example, at Motorola, the company's ethics and values are clearly covered in many of its training programs. Expectations are clearly understood by all employees, and infractions are punished. Sometimes that means a hard choice between doing something that will make money for the company—even though it is of questionable ethics—and forgoing such business opportunities. When being ethical is a widely known and accepted value of a corporate culture, such a choice is more easily made. As a director of education and training at Motorola has put it: "If we have to lose business, we lose business. People may feel that puts us at a competitive disadvantage. And that may be true. But we don't care to operate any other way."

Develop a means for discussing ethics

A second step to resolving ethical dilemmas is to have a means and strategy for deciding what is the "right" thing to do. Unfortunately, most issues in today's world are seldom black or white, and your choice of action will typically be among various shades of gray. These shades are lost when only quantitative analysis is made of potential business decisions. Reality is not so easily categorized and quantified. In fact, *sometimes when the numbers look right, the decision is still wrong.*

A useful guide that Norman Vincent Peale and I developed for our book *The Power of Ethical Management* suggests three questions that a person or group should ask when evaluating the ethics of a decision or potential action. We call these three questions the Ethics Check, and they are similar to guidelines recently developed by management at General Dynamics for all of its employees.

1. **Is it legal?** Will you be violating either civil law or company policy? This question gets you to look at existing standards.

2. **Is it balanced?** Is it fair to all concerned in the short term as well as the long term? Does it promote win-win relationships? This question activates your sense of fairness and rationality.

3. **How does it make you feel?** Will it make you proud? Would you feel good if your decision were published in the newspaper? Would you feel good if your family knew about it? This question focuses on your emotions and your own standards of morality.

238

I find the Ethics Check helps me gain perspective and provides an objective means for sorting the various dimensions of an ethical dilemma. It can easily be adapted to the decision process of almost any business problem, individually or in a group setting.

Acting on Your Good Intentions

If you are able to unravel an ethical dilemma, the even more challenging step is to act on what you believe to be the right thing to do. It is always easier to be ethical in theory and to fall back, in practice, to what is more convenient, more popular, or more lucrative, depending upon the circumstances of the situation. Being ethical, however, requires that you be committed, *especially* when it is not convenient, popular, or lucrative to do so.

Actions speak louder than words, and in organizations, actions serve as a role model for others to emulate. In a poll taken last year, 75 percent of people polled responded that the key characteristic they look for in a leader is *integrity*. At every conceivable opportunity, managers must show integrity by living up to the values and expectations of the organization.

The Five Principles of Ethical Behavior

You will be more likely to follow through on ethical behavior if you are prepared to act ethically. To me, this means having thought through the consequences of your actions in advance and having a firm conviction to act ethically *prior to facing a specific situation*. This means creating an image of yourself as an ethical person and having a plan to live up to that image. In the book *The Power of Ethical Management*, Norman Vincent Peale and I describe five principles that help us, over the long run, to live up to the ethical image we have of ourselves. We call these principles the Five Principles of Ethical Behavior. They are purpose, perspective, patience, persistence, and pride.

Essential to ethical behavior is an individual or organizational *purpose*—the mission of the person or company—that is

239

The Five Principles of Ethical Power for Individuals

1. **Purpose:** I see myself as being an ethically sound person. I let my conscience be my guide. No matter what happens, I am always able to face the mirror, look myself straight in the eye, and feel good about myself.

2. **Pride:** I feel good about myself. I don't need the acceptance of other people to feel important. A balanced self-esteem keeps my ego and my desire to be accepted from influencing my decisions.

3. **Patience:** I believe that things will eventually work out well. I don't need everything to happen right now. I am at peace with what comes my way!

4. **Persistence:** I stick to my purpose, especially when it seems inconvenient to do so! My behavior is consistent with my intentions. As Churchill said, "Never! Never! Never! Never! Give up!"

5. **Perspective:** I take time to enter each day quietly in a mood of reflection. This helps me to get myself focused and allows me to listen to my inner self and to see things more clearly.

simple, clearly stated, and guided by the values, hopes, and vision that help us determine acceptable and unacceptable behavior. An organization keeps to its purpose when work and life remain in *perspective* for employees. Managers and employees need to take time to pause and reflect, take stock of where they are, evaluate where they are going, and determine how they are going to get there.

Employees can keep to that purpose through a combination of *patience* and *persistence*. Patience is needed for employees to believe that holding to their ethical values will lead them to success in the long term. This involves maintaining a balance between obtaining results and caring how they achieve those results. Persistence involves having a commitment to live by ethical principles that does not falter over time.

When employees have patience and persistence in keeping to ethical principles they value, *pride* will result. They will feel proud of themselves and of their organization. When they feel this way, they can resist temptations to behave unethically.

In summary, the ethical implications of short-term business decisions have a long-term impact. A business can focus on the short-term, short-sighted goals of simply making money and, in the process, go out of business. In this manner, managing only for profit is like playing tennis with your eye on the scoreboard and not on the ball. It is, instead, in the best interest of business and managers in the long term—as well as the short term— to be ethical. This can best be done through establishing a code of ethics and a means for discussing ethical issues on a daily basis as business decisions are made.

References
and
Recommended Reading

Ackoff, Russell L. (1977). The Corporate Rain Dance. *The Wharton Magazine.* The Wharton School.

Adams, John D., editor. (1984). *Transforming Work.* Alexandria, VA: Miles River Press.

Adams, John D., editor (1986). *Transforming Leadership.* Alexandria, VA: Miles River Press.

Adams, John D. (August 1988). A Healthy Cut in Costs. *Personnel Administrator.*

Argyris, Chris & D. Schon (1978). *Organizational Learning: A Theory-in-Action Perspective.* Reading, MA: Addison-Wesley.

Autry, James A. (1991). *Love and Profit, The Art of Caring Leadership.* New York: William Morrow and Co., Inc.

Bateson, Gregory (1972). *Steps to an Ecology of Mind.* New York: Ballantine Books.

Bateson, Gregory (1979). *Mind and Nature: A Necessary Unity.* New York: E. P. Dutton.

Bateson, Gregory & Mary Catherine Bateson (1987). *Angels Fear: Towards an Epistemology of the Scared.* New York: MacMillian Publishing Co, Inc.

Bellah, Robert N., Richard Madsen, William M. Sullivan, Ann Swidler, & Steven M. Tipton (1985). *Habits of the Heart*. Berkeley, CA: University of California Press.

Bennis, Warren (1989). *On Becoming a Leader*. New York: Addison-Wesley.

Bennis, Warren & B. Nanus (1985). *Leaders*. New York: Harper & Row.

Blanchard, Kenneth & Spencer Johnson, M.D. (1982). *The One Minute Manager*. New York: William Morrow and Co., Inc.

Blanchard, Kenneth & Paul Hersey (1988). *Management of Organizational Behavior: Utilizing Human Resources*. Englewood Cliffs, NJ: Prentice-Hall.

Blanchard, Kenneth & Dr. Norman Vincent Peale (1988). *The Power of Ethical Management*. New York: William Morrow and Co., Inc.

Bohm, David (1980). *Wholeness and the Implicate Order*. London: Routledge and Kegan Paul Ltd.

Bradshaw, John (1988). *The Family*. Deerfield Beach, FL: Health Communications Inc.

Bradshaw, John (1988). *Healing the Shame that Binds You*. Deerfield Beach, FL: Health Communications Inc.

Bradshaw, John (1990). *Homecoming*. New York: Bantam Books.

Casti, John L. (1989). *Paradigms Lost*. New York: William Morrow and Co., Inc.

Davies, P. C. W. & J. R. Brown (1989). *The Ghost in the Atom: A Discussion of the Mysteries of Quantum Physics*. Cambridge, MA: Cambridge University Press.

Deforrest, Kathy (1984). The Art of Conscious Celebrations, in *Transforming Work*, editor John Adams, Alexandria, VA: Miles River Press.

DePree, Max (1989). *Leadership is an Art*. New York: Doubleday.

Eisler, Riane (1987). *The Chalice and the Blade: Our History, Our Future*. San Francisco: Harper & Row.

Forrester, J. W. (1965). A New Corporate Design. *Sloan Management Review*, MIT.

Frankl, Victor (1962). *Man's Search for Meaning: An Introduction to Logotherapy*. New York: Washington Square Press.

Freudberg, David (1986). *The Corporate Conscience, Money, Power, and Responsible Business*. New York: AMACOM, a division of American Management Association.

Fritz, Robert (1989). *The Path of Least Resistance*. New York: Ballantine.

Gardner, Howard (1983). *Frames of Mind: The Theory of Multiple Intelligences*. New York: Basic Books.

Galagan, Patricia (November 1989). Growth: Mapping Its Patterns and Periods, *Training and Development Journal.*

Gardner, John W. (1990). *On Leadership.* New York: The Free Press.

Garfield, Charles (1986). *Peak Performers, The New Heroes of American Business.* New York: William Morrow and Co., Inc.

Greenleaf, R.K. (1977). *Servant Leadership: A Journey into the Nature of Legitimate Power and Greatness.* New York: Paulist Press.

Harman, Willis (1988). *Global Mind Change: The Promise of the Last Years of the Twentieth Century.* Indianapolis, IN: Knowledge Systems, Inc.

Harman, Willis & Howard Rheingold (1984). *Higher Creativity, Liberating the Unconscious for Breakthrough Insights.* Los Angeles: Jeremy P. Tarcher.

Harman, Willis & John Hormann (1990). *Creative Work, The Constructive Role of Business in a Transforming Society.* Indianapolis, IN: Knowledge Systems, Inc.

Hutchins, Robert M. (1968). *The Learning Society.* New York: Praeger.

Imai, Masaaki (1986). *Kaizen, The Key to Japan's Competitive Success.* New York: McGraw-Hill.

Jaynes, Julian (1990). *The Origins of Consciousness in the Breakdown of the Bicameral Mind.* Boston: Houghton Mifflin

Koestler, Arthur (1959). *The Sleepwalkers.* Baltimore, MD: Penguin.

Korn/Ferry (1989). *Reinventing the CEO.* International and Columbia University Graduate School of Business.

Kuhn, Thomas (1970). *The Structure of Scientific Revolutions* (2nd ed.) Chicago: University of Chicago Press.

Land, George (1986). *Grow Or Die: The Unifying Principle of Transformation.* New York: John Wiley & Sons.

Levinson, Harry (1972). *Organizational Diagnosis.* Cambridge, MA: Harvard University Press.

Liebig, James E. (1990). *Business Ethics, Profiles in Civic Virtue.* Golden, CO: Fulcrum Publishing.

Maslow, Abraham (1971). *The Farther Reaches of Human Nature.* New York: The Viking Press.

McGregor, D. (1960). *The Human Side of Enterprise.* New York: McGraw-Hill.

Miller, L. (1984). *American Spirit: Vision of a Corporate Culture.* New York: William Morrow and Co. Inc.

Miller, William (1986). *The Creative Edge: Fostering Innovation Where You Work.* Reading, MA: Addison-Wesley.

Mollner, Terry (Jan. 1990). Making Employee Ownership Work, *Perspectives.* Burlingame, CA: World Business Academy.

245

Mollner, Terry (Winter 1991). The Psychological Shift Necessary for Employee Ownership to be Successful, *Perspectives*. Burlingame, CA: World Business Academy.

Morgan, Gareth (1986). *Images of Organization*. Beverly Hills, CA: Sage Publications.

Omhae, Kenichi (1990). *The Borderless World: Power and Strategy in the Interlinked Economy*. New York: HarperCollins.

O'Toole, James (1985). *Vanguard Management: Redesigning the Corporate Future*. Garden City, NY: Doubleday.

Parker, Marjorie (1990). *Creating Shared Vision*. Oslo, Norway: Norwegian Center for Leadership Development.

Peters, Tom (1987). *Thriving on Chaos, A Handbook for a Management Revolution*. New York: Harper & Row.

Peters, Tom & Robert H. Waterman, Jr. (1982). *In Search of Excellence, Lessons from America's Best-Run Companies*. New York: Harper & Row.

Peters, Tom & Nancy Austin (1985). *A Passion for Excellence, The Leadership Difference*. New York: Random House.

Prigogene, Ilya & Isabelle Stengers (1984). *Order Out of Chaos, Man's New Dialogue with Nature*. New York: Bantam Books.

Progoff, Ira (1963). *The Symbolic and the Real*. London: Coventure.

Ray, Michael & Rochelle Myers (1986, 1989). *Creativity in Business*. Garden City, NY: Doubleday

Renesch, John (July/August 1990). Paradigm Straddling Can be Painful for Everyone Involved, *The New Leaders*. San Francisco: Sterling & Stone, Inc.

Renesch, John (May/June 1991) Coming "Out of the Closet": A Time for Courage in the Workplace, *The New Leaders*. San Francisco: Sterling & Stone, Inc.

Sanford, Carol (1988). *The Culture of Continuous Improvement, Science into Technique*. Battleground, WA: Spring Hill Publications.

Sanford, Carol (1988). *The Scientific Basis of Developmental Organizations: Some Thoughts and Examples*. Battleground, WA: Spring Hill Publications.

Senge, Peter M. (1990). *The Fifth Discipline: The Art and Practice of the Learning Organization*. New York: Doubleday/Currency.

Sheldrake, Rupert (1981). *A New Science of Life: The Hypothesis of Formative Causation*. London: Blond and Briggs Ltd.

Sheldrake, Rupert (1988). *The Presence of the Past: Morphic Resonance and the Habits of Nature*. New York: Vintage Books.

Srivastva, Suresh, David Cooperrider, and Associates (1990). *Appreciative Management and Leadership, The Power of Positive Thought and Action in Organizations.* San Francisco: Jossey-Bass.

Theobald, Robert (1987). *The Rapids of Change: Social Entrepreneurship in Turbulent Times.* Indianapolis, IN: Knowledge Systems, Inc.

Thompson, John W. (1983). *The Human Factor: An Inquiry into Communication and Consciousness.* Farmingdale, NY: Coleman Publishing.

Tichy, N. M. & M. Devanna (1986). *The Transformational Leader.* New York: John Wiley & Sons.

Trachtenberg, Alan (1982). *The Incorporation of America: Culture and Society in the Gilded Age.* New York: Hill and Wang.

Vaill, Peter (1989). *Managing as a Performing Art.* San Francisco: Jossey-Bass.

Watson, John B. (1925). *Behaviorism.* New York: W. W. Norton.

Wilber, Ken, editor (1982). *The Holographic Paradigm and Other Paradoxes.* Boulder, CO: Shambhala.

Wilson, Larry (1987). *Changing the Game, The New Way to Sell.* New York: Simon & Schuster.

Zuboff, Shoshana (1988). *In the Age of the Smart Machine, The Future of Work and Power.* New York: Basic Books.

Zukav, Gary (1980). *The Dancing Wu Li Masters—An Overview of the New Physics.* New York: Bantam Books.

Zukav, Gary (1989). *The Seat of the Soul.* New York: Simon & Schuster.

How to Contact the Authors

Cynthia F. Barnum
Consulting Network Int'l, Inc.
244 West 72nd Street
New York, N.Y. 10023
(212) 362-4773

Ken Blanchard, Ph.D.
Blanchard Training & Development
125 State Place
Escondido, CA 92025
(619) 489-5005

Juanita Brown, President
Whole Systems Associates
166 Homestead Blvd.
Mill Valley, CA 94941
(415) 381-3368

Jim Channon
Balian Design Studios
P. O. Box 130
Hawi, HI 96719
(808) 889-0223

David R. Gaster
361-4 Post Road West
Westport, CT 06880
(203) 962-9338

Willis Harman, Ph.D.
c/o World Business Academy
433 Airport Blvd., Suite 416
Burlingame, CA 94010
(415) 342-2387

Charles F. Kiefer, Chairman
Innovation Associates, Inc.
P. O. Box 2008
Framingham, MA 01701
(508) 879-8301

Herman B. Maynard, Jr.
86 Sawin Lane
Hockessan, DE 19707
(302) 234-9791

William Miller
Global Creativity Corporation
453 Marin Drive
Mill Valley, CA 94941
(415) 388-7242

Terry Mollner, Ed.D., Chair
Trusteeship Institute, Inc.
23 Baker Road
Shutesbury, MA 01072
(413) 259-1600

Michael L. Ray, Ph.D.
Graduate School of Business
Stanford Univeristy
Stanford, CA 94305-5015
(415) 723-2762

Robert H. Rosen, Ph.D., President
Healthy Companies, Inc.
311 N. Jackson Street
Arlington, VA 22201
(703) 524-5797

Carol Sanford
Sanford and Ely Associates
28036 N.E. 212th Ave.
Battle Ground, WA 98604
(206) 687-1408

Peter M. Senge, Ph.D.
c/o Innovation Associates, Inc.
P. O. Box 2008
Framingham, MA 01701
(508) 879-8301

John W. Thompson, Ph.D., CEO
Human Factors, Inc.
4000 Civic Center Drive, Suite 302
San Rafael, CA 94903
(415) 499-8181

TO PURCHASE ADDITIONAL COPIES

of

New

Traditions

in Business

Spirit and Leadership in the 21st Century

Send your name, complete address, and check or money order for $25, which includes postage and handling, to:

World Business Academy

433 Airport Blvd., Suite 416

Burlingame, CA 94010

attn: *New Traditions in Business* **book**

THE NEW LEADERS

"This business publication is unique —it addresses many of the less-than-obvious factors in this rapidly changing world. It is essential for the thinking, creative and progressive business man or woman."

To subscribe:
Send your name and address and method of payment to the address below:

One year (7 issues) reg. $140 spl offer **$90**
Two years (14 issues) reg. $260 spl offer **$160**
Three years (21 issues) reg. $360 spl offer **$210**

By mail: *The New Leaders*
2115 Fourth Street
Berkeley, CA 94710

By FAX: 1-415-549-4331

By phone: 1-800-327-9893